# HEAL YOUR PAST
# AND CHANGE
# YOUR MARRIAGE

# HEAL YOUR PAST
# AND CHANGE
# YOUR MARRIAGE

## Paul and Kristina McGuire

HEAL YOUR PAST AND CHANGE YOUR MARRIAGE
by Paul and Kristina McGuire
Published by Creation House
A part of Strang Communications Company
600 Rinehart Road
Lake Mary, Florida 32746
www.creationhouse.com

Unless otherwise noted, all Scripture quotations are from the New King James Version of the Bible. Copyright © 1979, 1980, 1982 by Thomas Nelson, Inc., publishers. Used by permission.

Scripture quotations marked KJV are from the King James Version of the Bible.

Scripture quotations marked NAS are from the New American Standard Bible. Copyright © 1960, 1962, 1963, 1968, 1971, 1972, 1973, 1975, 1977 by the Lockman Foundation. Used by permission. (www.lockman.org)

Scripture quotations marked NEB are from the New English Bible. Copyright © 1961, 1970 by the Delegates of the Oxford University Press and the Syndics of the Cambridge University Press. Used by permission.

Library of Congress Cataloging-in-Publication Data:
McGuire, Paul 1953-
   Heal your past and change your marriage / Paul and Kristina McGuire.
     p. cm.
   ISBN: 0-88419-689-5
   1. Marriage-Religious aspects--Christianity. 2. Spouses--Religious life. 3. McGuire, Paul, 1953-4. McGuire, Kristina. I. McGuire, Kristina. II. Title.
BV4596.M3 M445 2000
248.8'44--dc21
                                                                    00-023251

0 1 2 3 4 5 6 VERSA 8 7 6 5 4 3 2 1
*Printed in the United States of America*

*To Paul, Michael and Jennifer*

*Thank you to all*
*the people at Creation House:*
*Stephen Strang, Dave Welday,*
*Rick Nash, Daphne Porter, Jay Griffin,*
*Mike Janiczek, Barbara Dycus and*
*Deborah Poulalion*

# Contents

# *Foreword*

NOTHING VERIFIES THE genuine practicality of biblical truth and Christian life like seeing it prosper in a marriage. By that measure, Paul and Kristina McGuire are living evidence that God's Word works!

I've been privileged to be called their pastor for more than a decade, and it's been gratifying to watch them grow. They've grown in Christ, in their life together, in their love for one another, and amid the whole, they've grown a happy family.

I've watched Paul become a *real* man. That's not an unkind commentary on his character or intentions before he realized this personal growth. It's simply to acknowledge this awesome, problematic truth: *None of us guys are real until the realities of godly manhood and being a Jesus-type husband grip our lives.*

I've watched Kristina become an increasingly secure, settled, solid and sensitive woman, wife and mother. I believe in the growth she and Paul have experienced and in the life they lead together.

*Heal Your Past and Change Your Marriage* offers realistic help to other couples. They point past the myth of a "perfect marriage" as they lead the way to real grounds for hope regarding struggles that marriage partners face. They address romance and the sexual aspects of our marriages, and they point the way to your home becoming a "powerhouse" through practical partnership in worshiping God (and keeping the Adversary off the premises!). This is big-time stuff!

Paul and Kristina have reason to be heard. . .or in this case, *read*. Help yourself to practical insight and hope-filled truth. The McGuires are here to join hands with you and, most importantly, to point you and your spouse toward partnering with the Ultimate Friend of marriages—Jesus, our Lord.

—JACK W. HAYFORD, PRESIDENT
THE KING'S SEMINARY
VAN NUYS, CALIFORNIA

# *Introduction*

WHILE DRIVING ON a freeway in Southern California, I read a bumper sticker that said, "Let's put the fun back in dysfunctional." I think it is important to say at the beginning that just because you came from a dysfunctional past does not mean you are doomed forever. With God all things are possible. You *can* have a meaningful and rewarding relationship with your marriage partner. With God on your side, you are not destined for a life of misery!

In Ken Kesey's powerful novel *One Flew Over the Cuckoo's Nest,* there is an opening poem that reads: "One flew east...one flew west...one flew over the cuckoo's nest."

In other words, your psychological past does not have to determine your future! When you receive Jesus Christ into your life, you are a brand-new creature in Christ. You do not have to settle for the marriage or relationship your parents had. You do not have to be trapped by the same forces that held your family in bondage. The blood of Jesus Christ and the power of the cross make it possible for you to inherit a brand-new way of living!

My own marriage is a testimony to the way God can heal your past and change your marriage. We believe with all our hearts that God honors marriage and makes a way through the Holy Spirit for couples to overcome their pasts and learn to love each other in the present.

This book is written for those who truly desire a breakthrough in their marriages and families. It does not promise to make your marriage perfect. But it does promise to show you how two imperfect people such as Kristina and myself were able to discover a deep and meaningful relationship.

Whether you need a romantic refresher or you're ready to call it quits, the principles in this book will take you to a new level in your relationship. May God bless you as you read and apply these words today.

# A Summer Poem for Kristina
## *by Paul McGuire*

*Ocean breezes*
*sweeping across*
*sun caressed sand;*
*A figure in the distance*
*looms upon the horizon—*
*It is you*
*in the distance.*
*Images play through my mind:*
*Ocean vessels,*
*sailboats from heaven,*
*blinding white light*
*spilling on the wind filled*
*sails.*
*Ocean breezes—*
*kinetic signals*
*of eternal love,*
*romantic love*
*for you,*
*the darling of my existence,*
*the desire of my eyes.*
*I see you coming up over*
*the dunes,*
*walking toward me.*
*Your eyes were filled with*
*light,*
*a light brighter than the*
*sun that lit up the day.*
*Then*
*an alarm clock blared*
*in disconcerting,*
*mechanized, coffee*
*machine hymns.*
*I awoke startled,*
*but then*

*I saw you beside me*
*gently sleeping,*
*and I fell into the oceans*
*of our love,*
*which came upon me*
*like the ocean's surf*
*in some lost world*
*of ancient paradise,*
*bathed in the glowing*
*waters of our love.*
*A midnight sun*
*dawned in the*
*Los Angeles morning,*
*spilling its light*
*over an ordinary*
*day,*
*transforming,*
*creating*
*a new splendor,*
*a new joy.*
*I watched you awake;*
*I saw you stir;*
*your eyes opened*
*and*
*the room disappeared.*
*Once again you were*
*walking toward me*
*on an eternal beach*
*bathed in light*
*with ocean breezes*
*rolling over my soul.*
*Your womanhood,*
*your femininity*
*restored me.*

*Like a modern Eve*
*walking backwards,*
*like being caught in*
*reverse search,*
*All the images*
*spilled backwards.*
*You retreated from*
*the apple;*
*the snake went out of*
*view;*
*the apple found its way*
*back onto the tree.*
*As the Lord's prayer*
*was uttered*
*the curse was undone,*
*and I looked back into*
*your eyes*
*as you walked upon the*
*eternal beach.*
*One glance from your*
*beautiful eyes*
*sent me flying*
*across time,*
*Back into paradise*
*where I walked with you*
*in the Garden*
*before time began.*
*And we heard*
*His voice together*
*and danced in His*
*Garden,*
*watching children play*
*in Paradise.*
*Another day in*
*Los Angeles*
*has begun.*

# Section I
# What Christian Marriage Is
# All About

# 1

## The Marriage
## That Almost Wasn't

I̲T WAS A beautiful wedding ceremony in a church. Kristina looked as beautiful and radiant as a bride could be in a wedding gown that a fashion designer friend had created especially for her. We shared communion together, and the gospel of Jesus Christ was communicated by the pastor performing the wedding to all who had gathered. A Christian singer sang songs of worship and praise.

At our reception we even had a scripture verse printed in gold lettering on the napkins: "How vast the resources of his power open to us who trust in him" (Eph. 1:19, NEB). We kissed at the altar and became husband and wife.

But what we didn't know at the time was that our

"Love Boat" was like the *Titanic*—ready to crash into a series of massive icebergs hidden below the surface at any time. In a nutshell, even though we were Christians, both of us were pretty messed up from our dysfunctional pasts. I didn't know that on the very day we were getting married Kristina had gotten up early to stuff and send dozens of envelopes with her picture and résumé to agents in Hollywood. She was so addicted to her career that even on her wedding day she was working on business.

Hours later that evening, during the honeymoon in a suite with a heart-shaped tub, our marriage almost ended in divorce. It wasn't that we were not passionately in love or that we didn't enjoy consummating our marriage physically. But the reality was that both of us brought a lot of extra baggage on our honeymoon—not suitcases full of clothes, but giant suitcases of emotional baggage from our dysfunctional pasts. Both of us came from family backgrounds where alcoholism, unfaithfulness, fear, depression and other factors were present.

Although there was passion, romance and a real spiritual commitment, there were also powerful forces that we were totally unprepared for at work tearing up our marriage. We both naively thought that if we were committed Christians, stayed sexually pure before our marriage and placed God in the center of our lives, then everything would be all right. What we didn't understand was that both of us came from alcoholic and dysfunctional homes that had constructed powerful strongholds in our personalities, which began to emerge as soon as we were married.

In addition, we had no positive role models or teaching on how to have a successful marriage. In a very real sense, we were thrown into marriage like lambs to the slaughter. As such, the early days of our marriage experience were like the Vietnam War with arguments, yelling and heated conflicts. To show you just how bad things were, we have a photograph of our marriage license that we ripped up soon after our marriage.

Kristina and I had absolutely no clue about how to resolve conflicts, communication, the different emotional needs of men and women or the proper spiritual roles the husband and wife must play in a marriage relationship. In addition, both of us had many issues from our pasts that needed to be healed and resolved.

At that time in our life I was the director of youth concerts at a "Christian nightclub" on Times Square in New York City. I had accepted Jesus Christ miraculously while hitchhiking on the back roads of Missouri. Jesus Christ delivered me from a lifestyle of drugs, drinking, sexual promiscuity, the New Age and radical politics. In any definition of the term, I could hardly be labeled Wally Cleaver from *Leave It to Beaver.* God had powerfully healed my life and had placed me in the first position of leadership I had ever had in my life.

However, the stress of New York City and the demanding schedule in being involved in a contemporary Christian music ministry where hundreds of people were accepting Jesus Christ and well-known singers were being flown in from around the nation began to hurt my already fragile marriage.

In addition, the little marriage advice I got from a well-meaning Christian leader was a recipe for disaster. He literally said to me, "You have got to grab the bull by the horns and show her who's boss." As a young husband who was totally ignorant about how to be an effective husband, I tried to assert my authority in an effort to save my marriage. I remember coming home one afternoon to our lovely newlywed apartment in Hoboken, New Jersey. I slammed a giant King James Bible down on the kitchen table and read Ephesians 5:22 to Kris: "Wives, submit yourselves unto your own husbands, as unto the Lord."

As you can imagine, my efforts actually made matters worse. After an argument, Kristina left me and returned to her hometown of Salt Lake City. Although neither she or her parents were Mormon, she grew up in this beautiful Rocky Mountain City, which was a distinct contrast to New York City.

In this moment of crisis I was faced with a decision to continue my ministry, which I felt would have been totally phony since my own personal life was in ruins, or to give up everything and pursue my wife. I chose to totally give up my career, leave everything I had and pursue my wife. Although I did not completely understand it at the time, I was fulfilling Ephesians 5:25 where it says, "Husbands, love your wives, just as Christ also loved the church and gave Himself for her." In addition, my decision to give up my life in order to save our marriage was in fulfillment of

John 15:13, "Greater love has no one than this, than to lay down one's life for his friends."

When I flew into Salt Lake City and Kristina met me at the airport, she was absolutely beautiful and more radiant than I had ever seen her. My giving up my interests and my career tripped some kind of switch in her heart and in the invisible realm. Deep healing began to flood through our lives, and we celebrated a second honeymoon that was much better than the first.

My willingness to obey God and leave everything for her released a powerful chain of healing in her life and in our marriage. During our arguments in New York City I was always reading to her Ephesians 5:22–23 and telling her to submit to me as the head of the home. Whenever I did this, she would rebel, and the conflicts would escalate. However, when I quit demanding that she be in submission to me and began laying my life down for her, then all of a sudden, she began submitting to me as head of the home. I began to discover that my authority as head of the home came from my willingness to be a servant.

God took a broken relationship and made something very beautiful out of it. Today, after twenty-three years of marriage and three wonderful children, we can say that we have a blessed marriage and a relationship of beauty—not a perfect relationship and not one without conflicts. But Kristina and I have learned how to become one, and we have discovered an intimacy and oneness that only God could have brought about.

In this book we will share some of the principles that

God has taught us, which can help turn any marriage around. No matter where you are in your marriage journey, there is hope and a promise of real restoration and healing. Perhaps the most important promise that God gave us in our marriage and that we want to share with you is from Joel 2:25–26:

> And I will restore to you the years that the locust hath eaten…And ye shall eat in plenty, and be satisfied, and praise the name of the Lord your God, that hath dealt wondrously with you: and my people shall never be ashamed.
>
> —KJV

**2**

# Imperfect People
# Who Love Each Other

I N THE EARLY days, when we were seeking help on how to find healing for our marriage, my wife and I bought several Christian books on marriage that actually made matters worse. These books were written for Mr. and Mrs. Perfect, which we definitely were not!

The marriage principles in this book are for people who are imperfect like us and who live in the real world and have real problems. I'm not Prince Charming, and my wife will tell you that she is not a storybook princess. Yet, as imperfect as we were (and still are), we discovered the amazing power of prayer and how to unlock powerful kingdom principles from the Bible on marriage and the family.

This book is written for imperfect people, singles, divorced and others who want to learn how God's Word and the power of prayer can transform a marriage and create a positive and healthy family. In a day when the phrase "family values" is talked about quite a bit, we must remember that almost 30 percent of all U.S. births are to single mothers. Households comprised of married couples with children represent only 26 percent of the general population. In contrast, in 1960, households comprised of married couples with children represented 44 percent of the population.

During World War II, 80 percent of children grew up in homes with two biological parents who were married to each other. In 1980 this figure had fallen to 50 percent. Today married couples with children make up only 26 percent of the U.S. population. There has been a 200 percent growth in single-parent homes since 1970 from 4 million to 8 million homes. The number of married moms leaving home for work each morning rose 65 percent from 10.2 million in 1970 to 16.8 million in 1990.[1]

These vital statistics provide real-world data about what is actually going on in the areas of marriage and family. Tragically, the failure rate for Christian marriages is in many cases as high as the secular society around it. The Barna Research Group, a respected Christian organization, conducted a sobering survey about Christian marriages in 1999. Among born-again Christians, 27 percent are currently or previously have been divorced, compared to 24 percent among adults who are not born again. Even without reading these statistics, all of us know of many Christian marriages and families, as well as non-Christian marriages and families, that have crumbled.

Yet in the midst of this social chaos and upheaval, God still has answers for both marriages and families. Ultimately, your marriage and family not only can work, but they can also be successful as you follow God's plan for marriage and families. As someone who has been there, I know first-hand that the principles in the Bible work and that it is possible to have a happy marriage and home in our modern pressure-cooker society.

In the final analysis, God established both marriage and the family as a unit. The Bible teaches us that when God calls us to do something, He always gives us the power to do it. Happy, prosperous and healthy families are possible even in today's hectic world because God has both the principles and the power to make them work if we choose to follow His plan for marriage and the family. The reason that the statistics for Christians regarding divorce and home life often parallel the society around them is not because God's plan for marriage does not work; it's because His principles are not being followed.

This book is about how you can discover the principles and the power from the Bible to make your marriage and family work. The good news is that even marriages in trouble can be healed and restored when they come into alignment with biblical principles. The Bible clearly tells how God established marriage, and we will look at those verses in the next chapter.

*3*

A Romance
at the Beginning
of Time

KRISTINA AND I had a "head-over-heels" courtship.
When we were first dating in Manhattan, it was a
very romantic time. We would walk through New York
City's Central Park holding hands. The beautiful trees, the
fountains and the lake in Central Park provided the back-
drop for much of our early courtship. We would stroll
together down 6th Avenue and Broadway, stopping to
share an Orange Julius orange drink together. We would
have dinner at "Ma Bell's" on Broadway. Then when all
of New York City was caught up in celebrating the 200th
birthday of our nation—and hundreds of sailing ships
filled the Hudson River while fireworks lit up the night
sky—we kissed each other.

The romantic and spiritual force that drew us together was the same attraction that men and women have felt since the dawn of time.

At the beginning of time, when God created the first man and woman, Adam and Eve, a romance existed that was far more wonderful than any modern soap opera or romantic novel could ever portray. Adam and Eve lived in a place called Paradise, which was more beautiful than the islands of Maui or Kauai with their lush gardens, brilliantly colored flowers and romantic waterfalls. Adam and Eve were in love from the first second they laid eyes on each other, and their passion and relationship deepened with every passing day.

In Genesis 1:26–28 we read:

> Then God said, "Let Us make man in Our image, according to Our likeness; let them have dominion over the fish of the sea, over the birds of the air, over the cattle, over all the earth and over every creeping thing that creeps on the earth." So God created man in His own image; in the image of God He created him; male and female He created them. Then God blessed them, and God said to them, "Be fruitful and multiply; fill the earth and subdue it; have dominion over the fish of the sea, over the birds of the air, and over every living thing that moves on the earth."

At the beginning of time, God placed a married couple at the very center of creation. In fact, Paradise was custom built and designed by God as a kind of endless honeymoon suite for Adam and Eve. This is really a very important point to grasp, because not only does this tell us that men and women are not the result of some kind of genetic alphabet soup spill as the theory of evolution suggests, but it also tells us that the wondrous married relationship between Adam and Eve actually is a perfect reflection or image of who God is.

At the very beginning of time God is saying that the marriage relationship between a man and a woman is a reflection of what is called the triune nature of God. When the Bible says things like, "Let Us make man in Our image" (Gen. 1:26), God was revealing to us His triune, or three-part, nature as God the Father and God the Son and God the Holy Spirit. The next verse reads, "So God created man in His own image; in the image of God He created him; male and female He created them" (v. 27). This verse reveals that the nature of God has both male and female characteristics, because male and female were both created in the image of God.

A married couple reflects the nature of God because they bring together both male and female characteristics, just as God's nature contains both male and female characteristics. In verse 26 the word *man*, or *Adam* in Hebrew, means man in the sense of both male and female. According to *The Spirit-Filled Life Bible, Adam* means mankind, humanity at large or the name of Adam, the first man.[1]

This is why the act of sexual intercourse is so sacred,

holy and profound. It initiates a deep oneness on both the biological and spiritual levels.

In addition, this is also why things like homosexuality are sins because they pervert or twist the original design of the image of God being reflected in both the male and female. Homosexuality is a complete misunderstanding of the basic design and purpose of men and women. It is forcing people to be something that they were not created to be.

At the very dawn of time God created man in His own image, and He established the institution of marriage and a family as the means of reflecting His nature. In this day of alternative lifestyles, nontraditional marriages comprised of homosexual relationships and people just living together or just "hanging out," we must realize that a heterosexual marriage between a man and a woman is not just some social institution invented by man or some evolutionary step in the continuation of the species. Marriage from the very beginning was God's idea and a special covenant relationship that God created.

When people in our contemporary society rebel against what is termed Judeo-Christian morality and the traditional family, they are, out of their ignorance and spiritual blindness, rebelling against God. Second Corinthians 4:3–4 gives us insight into how this spiritual blindness occurs: "But even if our gospel is veiled, it is veiled to those who are perishing, whose minds the god of this age has blinded, who do not believe, lest the light of the gospel of the glory of Christ, who is the image of God, should shine on them."

People who do not know Jesus Christ are blinded from the reality of what marriage is supposed to be all about. Tragically, they see marriage as some kind of outdated, man-made institution. They are missing out on the total wonder, discovery, romance and joy that is possible for those who have discovered what God had intended for those who live according to His marriage principles.

In the next chapter we'll see how God's plan for marriage creates a covenant that releases the husband and wife to enjoy the dance of life together.

*4*

................................................................

# The Marriage
# Covenant

ABOUT A YEAR after Kris and I were married, we ripped up our marriage license in the middle of one of our endless fights. I think she ripped it in half first, and then I grabbed it from her and tore it up myself. After coming to our senses some hours or days later (I can't remember), we taped it back together. But the reality was that in the heat of an argument, with tempers flared, we were ready to break our marriage covenant.

God set up marriage as a holy institution. Although modern man makes marriage into something casual or something that can annulled easily, God set up marriage as a covenant relationship. In Malachi 2:10–16 we learn a great deal about how God views marriage as a special covenant relationship. Let's look at the following verses, where God is speaking to the people of Judah about marrying people who worshiped idols:

> Why do we deal treacherously with one another by profaning the covenant of the fathers?
>
> —VERSE 10

> For Judah has profaned the LORD's holy institution which He loves.
>
> —VERSE 11

> Yet she is your companion and your wife by covenant.
>
> —VERSE 14

God's descriptive words about marriage teach us that the marriage relationship is a covenant relationship and a holy institution that the Lord loves. These are very powerful words.

If the Bible teaches us anything about the nature of God it is that He is a covenant-keeping God. Beginning in Genesis 3:15 we see that God is a Covenant-Maker. God made a covenant with Noah never to destroy the earth by a flood and gave the rainbow as a sign of this covenant (Gen. 9:8–12). Isaac was born as a result of a covenant God made with Abraham (Gen. 15:3–21; 21:1–3). In Genesis 15:10 we have the first blood sacrifice covenant. Then when Jesus Christ came, the New Testament (or covenant) was actuated. Matthew 26:28 is where Jesus inaugurates the New Covenant during a Passover meal.

From Genesis to Revelation we read constantly about the covenant relationship between God and His people. In the Old Testament the word *covenant* comes from the Hebrew word *berit,* which means "a pledge, treaty or agreement." According to the *The Spirit-Filled Life Bible*, "This is one of the most theologically important words in the Bible, appearing more than 250 times in the Old Testament."[1] When God made a blood covenant with His people, you can be sure that it was an agreement that could never be broken, because God's Word is absolutely true and unchangeable.

In the New Testament the word *covenant* comes from the Greek Word *diatheke,* which means "will, testament or pact." In the New Testament God ratified the New Covenant through the death of Jesus Christ on the cross. God's covenant with man is unshakable and cannot change. Therefore when God set up the holy institution of marriage, He set it up as a covenant relationship that was not designed to be broken.

In Ephesians 5:22–33 the apostle Paul describes the marriage relationship as representative of Christ and the church. Paul said specifically in verses 31–32:

> For this reason a man shall leave his father and mother and be joined to his wife, and the two shall become one flesh. This is a great mystery, but I speak concerning Christ and the church.

When believers in Jesus Christ get married, their

earthly marriage relationship reflects to the world the covenant relationship between Christ and the church.

Tragically, what many Christians in our day fail to realize and what large segments of the church at large have not understood is that our witness and ability to evangelize flow directly out of the faithfulness and quality of our marriage relationships. How can we share the good news of Jesus Christ and the reality of the New Covenant if we are breaking our marriage covenant, which is a direct reflection of the relationship between Christ and the church?

When Christians and the church attempt to witness for Christ in the context of broken marriage relationships where God's covenant and holy institution of marriage have been undermined, our witness not only lacks power and effectiveness, but it also rings hollow to a hardened and cynical world. The epidemic of divorce among Christian leaders and the church has seriously impacted our ability to influence our world for Jesus Christ. You cannot preach the gospel from a moral platform that has been eroded by divorce, adultery and deteriorated marriages.

It is not that God does not forgive people whose marriages end in divorce or who commit adultery—the blood of Jesus Christ cleanses every sin, and God can and does restore. People who have failed can be restored by the blood of Jesus Christ and returned to fruitfulness and ministry.

However, the casualness with which the church treats God's holy institution of marriage, which is a covenant relationship, is an indication that the spirit of the world has infiltrated the church.

Believers need to understand that marriage is a holy institution and a covenant relationship. Although the world through its celebrities promotes the idea of multiple marriages, casual relationships, extramarital affairs and no-fault divorce, believers are not to allow this form of the world spirit to enter their lives. For believers in Jesus Christ, marriage is to be a holy and pure covenant relationship of permanent commitment.

From this understanding, believers in Christ should enter into marriage as a lasting covenant relationship of total and complete commitment with no thought of divorce as a possible option. It should be viewed as a holy institution and a sacred covenant relationship.

However, it is important to add a word of caution. As with all of God's commandments and requirements, they are impossible to fulfill apart from a regular reliance on the power of the Holy Spirit. Otherwise you just have two people legalistically chained to each other in some kind of living hell. God is not looking for people who will endure each other and suffer through life together in a kind of legalistic obedience to Him. It is true that obedience to the marriage covenant requires a choice made by our wills. But it is not will power that will make God's plan for marriage happen anymore than our personal salvation can happen just through our human wills.

The joy, beauty and wonder of marriage can only be realized through the fresh infilling of the Holy Spirit. Two personalities can only enter the rich dimension of oneness along with its infinite possibilities through the indwelling of the Spirit of Jesus Christ filling the human personality. The marriage covenant should never be viewed as some kind of legalistic chain binding two people together out of fear, duty or obligation. It is a powerful, spiritual foundation of oneness that releases the husband and wife to enjoy the dance of life together.

We must remember that just as God's covenant relationship with man is based on love, the marriage covenant between a man and woman is based on love. It is love that binds a man and woman together, and it is love that will cause the marriage to blossom and flourish. No marital technique or course on effective communication can substitute for genuine love being expressed between two people in marriage. Because of the importance of love, the next chapter examines how people actually fall in love.

**5**

........................................

# Falling
# in Love

I REMEMBER WHEN I first noticed Kristina. I was watching a Christian play about Abraham and Sarah on stage at the Lamb's Club in New York. The Lamb's Club was a Christian "night club" and theater on Times Square where I worked as youth concert director and host of a contemporary Christian concert series that led hundreds of people to the Lord. The Lamb's Club was featured on the ABC television network. Even though I didn't know her name, as I was sitting there I couldn't help but notice that the girl who was playing Sarah had great legs. Sorry to burst some of your spiritual balloons, but the thing that first made me notice my future wife was her legs! Anyway, I decided then and there that I would find a way to meet that girl.

At first it was difficult, because every time I would try to go over to her and strike up a conversation, some other guy was always talking to her. Finally in desperation, I cornered her coming out of a New York deli directly outside the Lamb's Club Theater. She has just bought a mini-pecan pie. From there our relationship began.

In case some of you are tempted to dismiss me as some kind of lustful wretch with no spiritual discernment, as our relationship progressed, I began to realize that Kristina could very well be my future wife and that I had better commit this decision to the Lord. I literally laid down my romantic feelings toward Kristina and began to fast and pray for God's direction. I truly wanted God's will and not my own in choosing a wife. After much fasting and prayer, I felt a strong peace about my decision. I can also share that all the passions were strong in our courtship, but Kristina and I remained sexually pure and did not engage in any kind of sexual relations before our marriage.

The Bible teaches us that there are several different kinds of love. First, there is *phileo*, which is the kind of love a mother would have for her son, daughter or even a close friend. It is a brotherly kind of love from which we get the name of our modern city of Philadelphia. Second, there is *eros,* which is romantic or even sexual love. It is based on feelings of sexual and emotional attraction. Finally, there is *agape*, which is a totally selfless and God kind of love that can only be produced by the Spirit of Jesus Christ in a person's life. Therefore, when we talk about the word *love* we must remember the following three definitions:

1. *Phileo*—brotherly love; the love a mother has for her children
2. *Eros*—romantic or sensual love based on attraction and feelings
3. *Agape*—Christlike and selfless love characterized by giving

When we talk about love in our modern culture it is almost always in the senses of *phileo* or *eros*. Only Jesus Christ demonstrated what true *agape* love is by sacrificially dying on a cross for the sins of mankind. People who love others above themselves and give, expecting nothing in return, are loving in a Christlike or *agape* form of love.

When we use the phrase "falling in love," we are not referring to *agape* love but *eros*. The romantic love between a man and woman in our culture is based on emotional and physical attraction. It is a very powerful and almost mystical bonding force that brings two people together. However, in many respects it is a kind of illusion that is temporary and has no foundation to it. The reason so many marriages and relationships in our world break apart is because they are totally based on romantic love.

God created romantic love, or *eros*, as well as *agape*. In fact, God created the whole range of romantic, emotional and sexual responses between a man and woman. However, a lasting marriage or any relationship cannot be built on *eros* or the *phileo* kind of love. The kind of love that makes relationships, marriages and families stay together is *agape* love, and it is a fruit of the Spirit.

Galatians 5:22 states, "But the fruit of the Spirit is love..."

It is only the selfless and eternal love of Jesus Christ that can carry a marriage or a family through times of trial, adversity and challenge. Romantic love is a fickle kind of love; it does not have any staying power.

Let's look now at how the love teaching of 1 Corinthians 13 applies to the marriage relationship. Remember, love is the foundation of marriage.

- If I "have not love, I am nothing" (v. 2).
- "Love suffers long" (v. 4)—I am patient with my mate's imperfections.
- Love "is kind" (v. 4)—I seek ways to do good to my mate.
- "Love does not envy" (v. 4)—I will help my mate reach his or her potential.
- Love "is not puffed up" (v. 4)—I seek to serve and not be served.
- Love "does not behave rudely" (v. 5)—I am very sensitive to my mate's needs.
- Love "does not seek its own" (v. 5)—I love my mate with selfless *agape* love.
- Love "is not provoked" (v. 5)—I do not lose my temper under pressure.
- Love "thinks no evil" (v. 5)—I don't keep score of wrongs done to me.
- Love "does not rejoice in iniquity" (v. 6)—I don't delight in my mate's weaknesses.
- Love "rejoices in the truth" (v. 6)—I always believe the best about my mate.

- Love "bears all things" (v. 7)—I choose to respond in love and not anger.
- Love "believes all things" (v. 7)—I empower and release my mate to grow.
- Love "hopes all things" (v. 7)—I never give up on my mate, but I affirm him or her.
- Love "endures all things" (v. 7)—I remain committed to my mate in difficulty.
- "Love never fails" (v. 8)—In Christ love always wins over evil.

*Agape* love is the foundation for a Christian marriage. Romantic feelings come and go. The only real foundation for a Christian marriage is the *agape* or selfless love of Jesus Christ. We cannot produce this love by ourselves. It is only possible through a daily reliance on the Spirit's power. Any attempts to love our mates in our own strength with the kind of selfless love described above will result in burnout, depression and failure. The above task list is totally impossible without the Holy Spirit producing the fruit of the Spirit in our lives.

## ANATOMY OF ROMANTIC LOVE

Most marriages between a man and a woman begin with romantic love. First, there is some kind of physical attraction between the man and the woman. A man is usually physically attracted to the woman in some way by her appearance, eyes, hair, figure, clothes or some other physical feature. For the woman, the physical appearance may be important, but it is not as important as the emotional rapport that is developed between her and the man.

### *What turns a man on romantically*

1. *The physical appearance of the woman.* A woman does not have to be Miss America for a man to be attracted to her. But there must be something about the way she carries herself, her physical appearance, smile, countenance or figure that attracts a man. A man's primary romantic response is generated physically.

2. *The personality of a woman.* Men are attracted to different types of personalities in a woman— for example, the way she conducts herself, her sense of humor and her intelligence. But there must be something in the woman's personality that generates romantic excitement.

3. *The way the woman responds to the man.* Men are attracted to women who do not "throw themselves at them" but in some way meet the ego needs of the man. In her presence the man feels strong, energetic, intelligent and capable. In short, a man is "turned on" by a woman who makes him feel like a "real man."

### *What turns a woman on romantically*

1. *Sensitivity and emotional intimacy.* Unlike men, a woman's primary romantic trigger is not

necessarily the physical. Women still need to be attracted to a man on a physical level, but most women are more attracted to the sensitivity of a man and his ability to build emotional intimacy.

2. *Personality, sense of humor and intelligence of a man.* The main reason I fell in love with my husband, Paul, was not because he was handsome or intelligent (even though he was and still is). Quite honestly, in our early dating days, I thought he was way too serious. But then one day when we were talking, I saw a side of Paul that really attracted me to him—and that was his sense of humor. Paul was quick-witted and cracked a lot of jokes. It was Paul's sense of humor that really attracted me to him.

3. *Intimate communication, tenderness and sensitive romantic expressions of love* such as flowers, cards and notes. A woman becomes romantically turned on by creative expressions of love that reflect the man's sensitivity to her personal needs.

## THE BONDING PROCESS IN ROMANTIC LOVE

We can learn a lot about how to build a successful marriage by understanding the bonding process that occurs in romantic love. The Bible is light-years ahead of contemporary psychology in its understanding of the love between a man and a woman. Genesis 2:24 says, "For this cause a man shall leave his father and his mother, and shall cleave to his wife; and they shall become one flesh" (NAS). In a healthy marriage when a man and a woman have a baby, both parents start to bond with the little child. This bonding process consists of the following:

1. Regular eye-to-eye contact for long periods of time, sometimes seeming to stare endlessly into the child's eyes
2. Gentle expressions of physical touch such as caressing, tickling, patting, stroking, hugging and kissing; in many cases, breast-feeding by the woman
3. Verbal expressions of love such as saying "I love you" and making cooing noises; reassuring words and a gentle, loving tone in the voice
4. Regular playing with the infant
5. Smiling at the infant
6. Laughing with the infant
7. Generating a feeling of oneness where the parent loses his or her identity into that of the child

Obviously, in a healthy family the above forms of parent/child bonding would have occurred. When a man is attracted romantically to a woman and eventually gets married, he joins, or cleaves, to his wife. Part of this joining process is a new kind of bonding during the courtship process. If we examine the romantic bonding process during courtship, we will notice its similarity to the infant's bonding process with the parents. This is what is meant by Genesis 2:24 when it says, "Therefore a man shall leave his father and mother and be joined to his wife, and they shall become one flesh." In other words, the infant/parent bond is being replaced by the husband/wife bond. Although Genesis 2:24 refers to a man, much of the process would describe a woman also.

The end result of this romantic bonding is marriage, where the couple consummate the marriage in sexual intercourse and become one flesh. When Kris and I were dating, there was an intense bonding process. We would take the ferry from Manhattan to Staten Island. We climbed Bear Mountain and would have a Bible study on faith, hope and love. Walking around Broadway, we would stop in Nathan's and have a hot dog and soda. In the middle of all this activity, through casual conversation we opened our souls to each other. Here are the characteristics of the romantic bonding process during courtship:

1. Intense staring or gazing into one another's eyes for long periods of time, sometimes seeming to stare endlessly into one another's eyes

2. Gentle expressions of physical touch such as appropriate caressing, tickling, patting, stroking, hugging and kissing (For the Christian couple these activities will have clearly defined boundaries prior to marriage.)

3. Verbal expressions of love and affection such as "I love you"; reassuring words and a gentle, loving tone in the voice

4. Regular playing in activities that might seem ordinarily ridiculous for adults
5. Smiling together
6. Laughing together
7. Generating a feeling of oneness where the man and the woman seem to lose their identity in each other

Notice the similarity between infant/parent bonding and romantic bonding. God as the Master Psychologist designed the family unit to be a place of intense love, nurturing and bonding. When a child leaves his parents, he or she is then to begin a new bonding process with his or her mate. This is precisely why divorce is so devastating for children and adults—it literally tears in half the oneness that the bonding process builds. It leaves people feeling as if they have been ripped in half.

Divorce is a topic of much conversation in the Christian community today. Some would say that divorce is no big deal, but others are wondering why Christian marriages aren't doing better. Many times people will call the live radio talk show I host, called "Home Builders," with attitudes and ideas about marriage that I believe contribute to the culture of divorce within the church. In the next chapter I want to talk frankly about some of these attitudes in the Christian community that have tragically contributed to divorce between believers.

*6*

............................................................

# The Myth of the
# Perfect Marriage

A LOT OF PEOPLE have an idealized image or myth of what a perfect marriage should be. When Kristina and I were getting married, the television shows of our early childhood formed our expectations of what marriage should be about. We grew up watching programs like *I Love Lucy, Father Knows Best, Leave It to Beaver,* and *Ozzie and Harriet.* Although these were comedies, they presented a very charming picture of marriage. In today's culture, things have changed dramatically, but Hollywood still creates myths of a new kind of perfect marriage where romance, sex and affluence abound.

The stories of movie stars like Tom Cruise and Nicole Kidman, whose marriage has all the elements of a modern romance novel, capture the imaginations of a new generation. Tom Cruise and Nicole Kidman are very attractive, rich and very successful. As they jet across the globe and parade their sexuality in movies like Stanley Kubrick's *Eyes Wide Shut,* they present an image of marriage for the new millennium. Also, actor John Travolta and his wife fly by private jet across the world and present another picture of romance and success. Ironically, both of these couples are Scientologists. Their lifestyles are covered by every marriage and women's magazine and media outlet. Many young married couples secretly wish they could have a marriage and life just like theirs. But the problem is that the "perfect" marriages are media created and do not show the real stresses and problems.

Then when one of these perfect Hollywood marriages blows apart, like in the case of Demi Moore and Bruce Willis, everybody is shocked. All the wealth, fame and plastic surgery that Demi Moore had was not enough to keep their marriage together.

Larry Christenson, author of *The Christian Family* and chairman of the International Lutheran Renewal Center, gives us an insightful look into the nature of marriage when he writes:

> Successful marriage is not a business of perfect people living perfectly by perfect principles. Rather marriage is a state in which very imperfect people often hurt and humiliate one another, yet find the grace to extend forgiveness

to one another, and so allow the redemptive power of God to transform their marriage.[1]

Many of us have the mistaken idea that a successful marriage is a perfect marriage. This is especially true in the Christian community where we often feel the pressure to be perfect people. The only problem is that none of us are perfect people, and as such, none of our marriages will be perfect. Occasionally I have met people who have appeared to have the perfect marriage, family and relationship. However, without exception, the closer I got, the more I could see the flaws and imperfections.

Unfortunately, especially in religious circles, the pressure to maintain a facade of being perfect in our own personal behavior and marriage can become unbearable. This pressure and false expectation of having to be perfect in order to be accepted is not only unbiblical, but it also leads to all kinds of problems, including nervous breakdowns, divorce and leaving the church. The bottom line is that all of us are sinners saved by grace.

If we understand the reality that we are indeed imperfect people and that our marriages will be imperfect, we can be set free from the disillusionment and despair that false expectations can often bring. Also, when we understand that it is impossible to achieve the perfect marriage, then we can be free to be thankful for and enjoy the imperfect marriages that we do have. When people say that they have the "perfect marriage," they may mean well, but red flags should go off at a statement like that. None of us have arrived, and each of us is in the process of redemption. It is a freeing thing to realize that we can have good and even great marriages without having to be perfect.

Commenting about this false ideal of perfection in both families and marriages, Dr. Francis Schaeffer writes in his book *True Spirituality*:

> One does not need to have had much pastoral experience to have met married couples who refuse to have what they can have, because they have set up for themselves a false standard of superiority. They have set up a romanticism, either on the side of romantic love or the physical side, and if their marriage does not measure up to their own standards of superiority, they smash everything to the ground. They must have the ideal love affair of the century because of who they are! Certainly multiple marriage and divorce situations turn upon this point. One couple refuses to have less than what they have set as a romantic possibility, forgetting that the Fall is the Fall. Another may want to have a sexual experience beyond what one can see in the midst of the results of the Fall. You suddenly see a marriage smashed—everything gone to bits, people walking away from each other, destroying something really possible and beautiful—simply because they have set a proud standard and refuse to have the good marriage they can have.[2]

Dr. Schaeffer gives a rich understanding into one of the most important factors contributing to divorce in our time— the false standard of perfection. In our modern culture this false concept of perfection drives many of the media super-stars in film, television and records to move from one relationship to another. Often these people seem to "have everything"—physical looks, money, power and the world basically at their feet. Yet they move from relationship to relationship every couple of years. The reason is that once the romantic high is over and the heady rush of romantic infatuation leaves, they have nothing left.

Tragically, many in the church of Jesus Christ are looking for this perfect relationship because this world's mind-set has infiltrated their thinking. For the Christian there is a basic reality concerning life, marriage and family. Life as we know it is being experienced after the Fall of man in the Garden of Eden. In other words, everything in our present reality is imperfect. Although Jesus Christ has redeemed us by His blood, our actual lives are in the process of redemption. Therefore our bodies, minds, marriages and families are not perfect.

There is nothing wrong with attempting to improve our marriages and families. However, if we are striving for perfection, we are only going to drive ourselves crazy. There are a lot of secular authors who write books that make false promises of total relational and marital bliss and tell us that we are dysfunctional if we do not achieve a kind of marital paradise here on earth. This is a deceptive lure and based on half-truths. If you investigate the hidden reality of many of secular society's most prominent "experts" on relationships, marriage and family, you will discover that they have had—and continue to have—multiple marriages and relationships. One of the most famous secular authors on the family and healing is recently divorced, and another who advises millions on marriage, relationships and children was married only briefly, has never had children and continues to have a series of short-term relationships with various boyfriends. I point this out not to convey a tone of moral superiority, but simply to suggest that many of these people who talk about an unrealistic ideal have not been able to reach it themselves.

## THE TRAGEDY
## OF CHRISTIAN DIVORCE

A couple of years ago I was walking through the hotel lobby of a convention where I was speaking and saw an old friend from a Christian media company. I asked him how things were going and how his wife was. He said, "Oh, don't you know? My wife and I got divorced about a year ago. After the divorce, I ran into my high school sweetheart, and we are married now." Although I was outwardly polite, I felt as if my heart were stabbed with a knife. *What a tragedy!* I thought to myself.

Please don't misunderstand me, because I didn't relate that story to convey any spiritual superiority. Believe me, I fully understand that it is only by God's grace that I have been married to my one wife for more than twenty-three years. However, there have been so many Christians who have divorced that it tears at my heart. I personally know, as I am sure you do, of many Christians who have divorced. Even in Christian leadership, the landscape is filled with pastors, evangelists, Bible teachers, speakers, authors and musicians who have divorced, and some who have been exposed for immorality.

The great tragedy is that the pressures of our modern society, along with the world spirit of this age, have taken their toll on believers in Jesus Christ. It's not that God cannot forgive people and restore them, because He certainly does. I know of excellent men and women of God who have either gotten divorced or failed morally and have been completely forgiven and restored. Many of these people have now become some of the strongest Christians I know. Yet it is never God's purpose and plan for people to get divorced, and much pain and suffering could be avoided if His ways were followed.

Malachi 2:13–16 gives us some insight into God's attitude toward divorce:

> And this is the second thing you do: You cover the altar of the LORD with tears, with weeping and crying; so He does not regard the offering anymore, nor receive it with goodwill from your hands. Yet you say, "For what reason?" Because the LORD has been witness between you and the wife of your youth, with whom you have dealt treacherously; yet she is your companion and your wife by covenant. But did He not make them one, having a remnant of the Spirit? And why one? He seeks godly offspring. Therefore take heed to your spirit, and let none deal treacherously with the wife of his youth. "For the LORD God of Israel says that He hates

divorce, for it covers one's garment with violence," says the LORD of hosts. "Therefore take heed to your spirit, that you do not deal treacherously."

These are very strong words from God. God clearly states, "For the LORD God of Israel says that He hates divorce, for it covers one's garment with violence" (Mal. 2:16). Divorce not only hurts men, women and children at the deepest levels of their being, but it also creates a ripple effect in society, spreading pain, dysfunction and chaos wherever it happens.

God speaks very directly to men when He reminds them that He will ignore their offerings and prayers if they are not treating their wives properly. The apostle Peter reinforces this theme when he writes, "Husbands, likewise, dwell with them [your wives] with under-standing, giving honor to the wife, as to the weaker vessel, and as being heirs together of the grace of life, that your prayers may not be hindered" (1 Pet. 3:7). If a man is not relating to his wife properly, God promises to hinder or not answer all of his prayers.

The powerful truth in Malachi regarding divorce is tar-geted toward men. God holds men responsible for the following things in the marriage relationship:

1. Dealing improperly or "treacherously" with your wife; doing anything that causes her to feel badly

2. Breaking the marriage covenant by being unfaith-ful in thought-life or in the real world

3.  Maintaining the right attitude toward their wives. Ephesians 5:25–33 tells men to cherish, nourish and love their wives as they do ourselves.

One of God's original purposes and primary goals in the marriage relationship is to produce godly offspring or children. Genesis 1:28 says, "Then God blessed them, and God said to them, "Be fruitful and multiply; fill the earth and subdue it." Malachi 2:15 says, "He seeks godly offspring." When men violate the marriage covenant and divorce their wives or become unfaithful, this child-rearing process is either stopped or hindered by the great emotional damage done to the children. God hates that. Divorce disintegrates the healthy family environment that builds spiritually and emotionally strong boys and girls.

What it boils down to is this: Divorce is always God's second best. Divorced people can be forgiven, restored and active in God's work, but the effects of what they have done will remain always. Let's stop chasing the myth of perfection and learn to enjoy what God has given us.

Perhaps the best way we can learn to enjoy the marriage God has given us, to stop chasing perfection and to head off divorce is to understand how strongholds from our past can often block our present success in marriage. The negative memories and experiences from our past can keep us in emotional and spiritual prisons that can destroy the joy and fulfillment that God intends for us in marriage. We must understand that not one of us is in our marriage alone. The God who created marriage can give us the power to live our marriages successfully. He has the power to take the pain of our pasts and transform it into something beautiful.

# Section II
# Fighting for Your Marriage in the Spirit

# 7

## Hell in Hoboken

I MET KRISTINA IN New York City while promoting a Christian theater production in the Broadway theater district. Kristina was acting in a Christian theater production called "Bright New Wings." I asked her out, and we immediately fell in love. After dating for about nine months, we got married.

Shortly after Kristina and I got married, we moved to Hoboken, New Jersey.

At that time Hoboken, which is just a few minutes away from Manhattan, was supposed to be a trendy and "artsy" place to live. Filmmakers like John Sayles lived there, and two friends of ours who were contemporary Christian musicians convinced us to live there.

Trendy or not, Hoboken was a depressing place to live. As a youth minister with a ministry called the "Lamb's Club," I didn't make a lot of money, so we rented an apartment on the top floor of a house. Below us lived the three elderly ladies who owned the house.

Almost immediately after we moved in, World War III started in our relationship, and we fought like cats and dogs. We yelled, screamed and argued constantly.

To compound the pain, we both felt guilt and shame about our behavior because this was not how "real Christians" should act. Whenever our arguments got especially loud, one of the old ladies would take a broom handle and knock on her ceiling, which happened to be our floor, with a loud series of thuds. This was their signal for us to quiet down. Although hundreds of people were coming to Jesus Christ through the concert ministry I hosted on Times Square every week, my private life was like being in a living hell. We felt like characters trapped in a bizarre existential play like Jean Paul Sartre's *No Exit.*

What neither of us understood at the time was that we were simply reenacting the behaviors both of us saw modeled by our parents in childhood. Clearly, we both had the power to choose to behave differently than our parents did, and we are not trying to use our parents as scapegoats. But you don't walk into a marriage with deep unresolved issues from the past and expect everything to go blissfully. Like the story of the *Titanic,* there are huge icebergs hidden beneath the surface that will destroy our relationships if they are not properly dealt with.

Today our experience is not all that uncommon. Millions of people now entering marriage come from broken and dysfunctional homes. We live in a world where healthy marriages are not all that common. Many people are carrying with them destructive issues from their pasts that are going to affect their relationships unless they find healing.

Both Kristina and I carried into our marriage relationship the painful memories of our pasts. Kristina had a bad relationship with her mother. As such, she was filled with anger, resentment and unforgiveness.

She also did not have a healthy relationship with her father, who was her primary male authority figure, and this carried over into her relationship with me.

In addition, my relationship with my father was very poor. He was abusive and often critical of me when I was growing up, and I did not sense his acceptance or affirmation. Because of this, beneath the cynical and macho facade I tried to put up was a frightened, insecure and confused little boy. My father also had a series of relationships with women and a number of wives. He was a heavy drinker as well as an artist. The image of manhood he modeled for me was the "conquest of women as sexual objects"—kind of like the way you would score points in a basketball or football game. I carried into my marriage unforgiveness toward my father, rage, anger, depression and other unresolved issues.

When Kristina and I got married, both of us were like

ticking emotional time bombs ready to explode. Yet no one told us or counseled us about what was going to happen. The Christian marriage books we read were like Betty Crocker instant cake mixes. They offered quick advice that did not deal with the root issues in people's lives.

However, there was one Counselor to whom we could turn, and that was Jesus Christ. In our pain and agony we called upon God to help us. Although He did not solve our marriage problems overnight, He was faithful to begin a healing work in our personalities and marriage. Although it did not seem like it at the time, Jesus Christ began to do a deep healing work in our lives. He walked us through the often slow and painful process of growth and healing.

## MARRIAGE COUNSELING IN THE HEAVENLIES

It seems difficult to go to God in prayer when everything seems to be going wrong in your marriage. However, every time we go to God in prayer, we are responsible to exercise at least a mustard seed of faith. In the face of marital and relationship difficulties, a mustard seed may be all we have. Yet Hebrews 11:1 teaches us the principle that is at work: "Now faith is the substance of things hoped for, the evidence of things not seen."

In the middle of seemingly insurmountable marriage difficulties, when you may be tempted to say, "I want out!", we can come to God with our small mustard seed of faith. On the basis of the promises in His Word, we can ask Him to transform and heal the marriage. It is through faith in God's power and not our own that we can believe that He can turn a bad situation around, and He can! When the outward reality is one of seemingly hopeless conflict and an endless cycle of arguments, it may appear hopeless from our limited human perspective. However, through eyes of faith we can see that if we ask Him in prayer, God can and will turn things around.

I remember many times while jogging in the foothills of Monrovia, California, going to God in prayer and bringing myself and Kristina into the throne room of God and placing our marriage before God's throne. I would do this over and over again by faith, in prayer asking God to heal our lives and our marriage.

Hebrews 10:19–22 says, "Therefore, brethren, having boldness to enter the Holiest by the blood of Jesus, by a new and living way which He consecrated for us, through the veil, that is, His flesh, and having a High Priest over the house of God, let us draw near with a true heart in full assurance of faith, having our hearts sprinkled from an evil conscience and our bodies washed with pure water." Because of the blood of Jesus Christ we can go directly into the throne room of God to receive healing for our marriages and our lives. We can come into the presence of God even though we may have sinned, lost our tempers and said the wrong thing. If we ask Jesus for forgiveness, we are washed in His blood.

It is interesting to note that Paul's marriage instructions in Ephesians 5:26 uses the phrase "that He might... cleanse her with the washing of water by the word" and that Hebrews 10:22 uses the expression "our bodies washed with pure water." In both cases the Bible makes reference to the cleansing that Jesus Christ makes possible for believers by His blood. Because Jesus makes us pure, we can go to God without hesitation in prayer.

Supernatural power from heaven is available to heal our marriages and lives. We may find ourselves in what seems like hopeless conflicts, situations and problems. But if we go to God in prayer, He promises to change things and heal us. It may not happen overnight, and it may take years for us to see the complete changes we want. But one thing we must realize is that marriage is God's idea—not man's. God not only created the institution of marriage, but He also promises to send us the power to make our marriages work.

Throughout the Bible God calls His people to do many things that are quite impossible to achieve through their own strength and ability. A true Christian marriage, like the Christian life itself, is impossible to live without daily relying on the Spirit's power. It requires dying to self by the Spirit's power and being resurrected by the Spirit's power.

As believers in Jesus Christ we need to come to the place where we really realize that it is impossible to live the Christian life, bear the fruit of the Spirit, reach the lost, fulfill our ministries and have the kind of marriage the Bible calls for without the power of the Holy Spirit. In all those cases, we may think we can fake it and do it by ourselves. But the way God constructed the Christian life and marriage to work, it just doesn't function without the power of the Holy Spirit anymore than a car can run without gas.

In fact, I believe one of the most important practices in a thriving marriage is spiritual warfare. You can't blame all marital conflict on the devil, but you can be sure that Satan hates a strong marriage and will seek to harm it. The next chapter gives you ten strategies for doing battle for your marriage in the spiritual realm.

*8*

.................................................................................................................

# Spiritual Warfare
# in Marriage

S HORTLY AFTER WE were married, Kristina and I were
having an argument in front of where we lived in
Hoboken, New Jersey. I don't know if any of you have
ever seen the Western movie *High Noon* where a huge
gunfight occurred just before noon in the town. Well,
Kristina and I were having a verbal shootout in the middle
of the street—except it wasn't at noon, but close to midnight! Kristina told me that she was going to leave me, so
with a desperate bravado, I told her that she better be
careful because I was going to be a movie producer and
she would not be able to star in any of my movies. That
was a pretty big boast from a guy who couldn't afford to
buy a Subway sandwich. (By God's grace, however, I did

produce a few feature films in which Kristina starred.)

The devil was trying to destroy our marriage, and we didn't have a clue about what to do about it. To give you an idea of how confused and distorted our spirituality was, I once left Kristina at the Port Authority bus station so I could rush home to watch Billy Graham on TV. For those of you who have never been there, the Port Authority in New York City is one of the most awful places on the face of the earth. Prostitutes, criminals, serial killers and drug addicts hang out in this bus terminal. I was in such a hurry to get a "blessing" and grow spiritually that I left her in this hell hole so I could rush home and listen to Billy Graham preach.

The devil takes full advantage of our misguided spirituality. Many Christian marriages come under attack when a misguided husband or wife prioritizes church or prayer meetings over their marriage.

To my knowledge I have never read a book on marriage that dealt with the need for and the reality of spiritual warfare in marriage. As Christians, when we are married and have families, we will be attacked by an unseen adversary, and we need to know how to wage spiritual warfare against this adversary.

First of all, the entire flow of the world system is often against things like virginity, marriage, sexual purity, monogamy, traditional family values and even heterosexuality. These virtues are attacked because they represent God's plan for mankind. As the Bible teaches us, there is a revolution against God's divine order that is being led by Satan and his demons: "And war broke out in heaven: Michael and his angels fought with the dragon; and the dragon and his angels fought, but they did not prevail, nor was a place found for them in heaven any longer. So the great dragon was cast out, that serpent of old, called the Devil and Satan, who deceives the whole world; he was cast to the earth, and his angels were cast out with him" (Rev. 12:7–9).

We learn a number of things from this passage. First, there is the ever-present reality of conflict in the invisible realm. Second, there is a battle between God and His angels and Satan and his demons. It is interesting to note that this "great dragon" or "the serpent of old" (Satan) is the same being who attacked the first marriage and family in the Garden of Eden. This "serpent of old" seduced Adam and Eve into disobeying God, which resulted in the Fall of Man (Gen. 3:1–6).

The reason the feminist movement, the gay rights movement, pornography and the modern social engineering by the elite all attempt to destroy the family is because ultimately they are part of a revolution against God spawned by powerful forces in the invisible realm. In fact, the whole anti-family nature of much of contemporary culture is the result of a very real antichrist spirit that is at work. The apostle John warns us to guard against ideas and beliefs that oppose God's Word and are motivated by the spirit of the Antichrist (1 John 4:1–6).

The very existence of the modern Christian marriage and family is a powerful testimony to the watching world of the reality and lordship of Jesus Christ. Christian marriages where the husband and wife truly love each other and Christian families that are whole and functional proclaim strong evidence that the God of the Bible really exists. It is precisely for this reason that Satan hates both marriage and family and seeks to destroy them.

The reality of spiritual warfare in the lives of married Christians is not a reason to blame all marital conflict or problems on the devil. Many marriage and family problems are due to self-centeredness, ignorance and sin. However, it is important to exercise real spiritual discernment and understand that there are times when conflict and problems are not just on the human level, but they are actual assaults from hell. In other words, powers of darkness may attempt to strike the Christian marriage and family and may be active in marital discord, temptations to infidelity, confusion, strife, financial problems and sickness.

The apostle Paul gives us instructions on how Christians can stay prepared to win victory over this unseen adversary:

> Finally, my brethren, be strong in the Lord and in the power of His might. Put on the whole armor of God, that you may be able to stand against the wiles of the devil. For we do not wrestle against flesh and blood, but against principalities, against powers, against the rulers of the darkness of this age, against spiritual hosts of wickedness in the heavenly places. Therefore take up the whole armor of God, that you may be able to withstand in the evil day, and having done all, to stand.

> Stand therefore, having girded your waist with
> truth, having put on the breastplate of righteousness,
> and having shod your feet with the preparation of
> the gospel of peace; above all, taking the shield of
> faith with which you will be able to quench all the
> fiery darts of the wicked one. And take the helmet of
> salvation, and the sword of the Spirit, which is the
> word of God; praying always with all prayer and
> supplication in the Spirit.
>
> —EPHESIANS 6:10–18

Any Christian marriage or family where Jesus Christ is being glorified and the testimony of Christ is going forth is going to be attacked or challenged sooner or later. This is not a call to paranoia or an excessive interest in demons. It is simply an acknowledgment of the reality of spiritual conflict in the life of every believer. There are a number of things a husband and wife can do along with their children to keep their spiritual defenses strong.

## TEN STRATEGIES FOR SPIRITUAL VICTORY

1. The husband and wife should pray and read their Bible together on a regular basis. If they have children, then the children should be part of the devotional life.
2. The husband and wife along with their family should be submitted members of a local Bible-believing church.
3. The husband should be the priest of his home and should pray for his wife and family daily.

4.  The power of regular praise and worship should be released in the household with Christian music and praise and worship aloud in times of regular devotions. (You will read more about worship in the next chapter.)

5.  The power of blessing should be released on the marriage and the household with the husband and wife speaking blessing on each other and the children.

6.  The husband and wife should engage in regular times of communion.

7.  The blood of Jesus Christ should be appropriated with its power released to break bondages and forgive sins.

8.  The husband and wife should pray specifically against the powers of darkness operating in their lives and the lives of their children.

9.  Generational problems or curses such as alcoholism, sexual disorder, molestation and other dysfunctions should be broken through intercessory prayer.

10. There must be a constant infilling of the Holy Spirit in the life of the marriage and family to refresh, heal, restore and empower.

While all of these strategies are important, the next chapter will go into detail about one—worship—and how it can change your marriage.

*9*

········································

# The Priority of
# Worship in Marriage

O NE MORNING KRISTINA and I were arguing as we were driving to church. There was a lot of hostility in the air. I think there are special demons assigned to attack believers as they are trying to go to church. However, the minute we walked through the sanctuary we could feel the presence of the Lord. In an instant, the strife and tension were broken off of us as we were bathed in the presence of the Holy Spirit. The worship that was going on in the sanctuary invited the presence of God.

At the core of any marriage should be a husband and wife who worship the Lord from the very center of their beings. John 4:23–24 says, "But the hour is coming, and now is, when the true worshipers will worship the Father in spirit and truth; for the Father is seeking such to worship Him. God is Spirit, and those who worship Him must worship in spirit and truth." When a husband and wife worship God from the very center of their lives, they will discover that their marriage, family and home begin to be completely transformed. Heaven is no longer far away and distant, but a very real taste of heaven emerges in their midst.

Worship is not just something you do when everything is going all right. A husband and wife must learn the warfare of worship and must worship God even in difficult times. Satan seeks to come in with outside pressures, turmoil and strife. Yet the worship of God's people literally drives the enemy back and causes the kingdom of God to be advanced in their lives.

A healthy family is one where the worship of God is freely manifest. Dysfunctionality, despair, negativity and pain cannot coexist with the worship and praise of God's people. We must learn to see that worship is not just a religious duty but a powerful dynamic that releases God's majesty and presence in the midst of our lives. The husband and wife must begin to worship God unabashedly and praise the Lord aloud. In Ephesians 5:18–19 Paul describes the main characteristics of the Spirit-filled marriage: "And do not be drunk with wine, in which is dissipation; but be filled with the Spirit, speaking to one another in psalms and hymns and spiritual songs, singing and making melody in your heart to the Lord."

Worshiping God in our hearts, singing to the Lord,

praising God aloud, speaking to one another in psalms, hymns and spiritual songs and making melody in our hearts to the Lord release the blessing of God in our lives in a way that nothing else can. The very center of our marriages must be filled with rich praise to God, for it is only the worshiping marriage that can experience the fullness of God's blessing.

Worship and praise release God's angelic forces, His supernatural power, His healing and His grace. No matter what trial, temptation or adversity we are experiencing, the joy of the Lord can be restored and victory gained when we worship God.

In our marriages our attention should never be on our lack, our problems or our hurts. We must release those things to God and enter His courts with thanksgiving and praise. As we do this, a supernatural dynamic is released. The fountain of life bubbles up in our inner being. As the living water builds up in our inner personalities, it puts pressure on the outer circumstances that are attempting to crush us. Worship to God provides release and deliverance for our marriages and lives.

The keys to releasing worship in our marriages are as follows:

1. Praise God aloud in our homes, cars and other places.
2. Be thankful to God for everything.
3. Sing to God.
4. Rejoice in the Lord regardless of circumstances.

5. Speak in our heavenly language.
6. Lift up our hands in worship.
7. Declare God's victory ahead of time.

Worship and praise in marriage are absolute essentials in realizing the kind of marriage that God has in mind for you. You can read books on marriage by the dozens, discover strongholds in your past and endlessly try to change your behavior and communicate better. But unless you praise and worship God as a regular part of your lifestyle, the power will never be released to bring you into the promised land of a fulfilled marriage. Worship and praise always precede victory. As a husband and wife we must learn the discipline of praising God even if we don't feel like it or if the circumstances are negative. Our obedience in praising and worshiping God will drive hell out and bring heaven down.

# 10

## The Pruning
## Process

ONE OF THE early comedians of late-night television was Milton Berle.

Milton Berle used to make a famous joke about a town
called Cucamonga in California. When Kristina and I first
moved to Southern California, we actually lived in Cucamonga. The real estate developers changed the name
slightly to give a more upscale ring to it by calling it
Rancho Cucamonga, but it was still Cucamonga.

The Lord taught us some powerful lessons in Cucamonga. We had moved to Cucamonga from Salt Lake City
where the Lord first began healing our marriage.

We chose to go to California primarily to be in the entertainment industry. I had already produced an independent

feature film that Kristina starred in, and we thought we would come to California to get into the film business in a bigger way. However, we were also committed Christians, and the Lord had directed us to become part of The Church On The Way in Van Nuys, California. So every Sunday we would drive about one hour and forty-five minutes each way to go to The Church On The Way in Van Nuys.

Living out in Cucamonga, we were somewhat isolated and cut off from Los Angeles. All around Rancho Cucamonga were vineyards where we jogged around for miles. As we jogged, we often noticed that the vines were cut back and pruned for greater fruitfulness. The Lord spoke to us and told us that He was pruning our lives for greater fruitfulness at that time. Although it was a painful time, we knew we were being cut back or pruned for a plan and a purpose.

In John 15:1–8 Jesus Christ outlines this principle of fruitfulness for His disciples:

> I am the true vine, and My Father is the vine-dresser. Every branch in Me that does not bear fruit He takes away; and every branch that bears fruit He prunes, that it may bear more fruit. You are already clean because of the word which I have spoken to you. Abide in Me, and I in you. As the branch cannot bear fruit of itself, unless it abides in the vine, neither can you, unless you abide in Me. I am the vine, you are the branches. He who abides in Me, and I in him, bears much fruit; for without Me you can do nothing. If anyone

does not abide in Me, he is cast out as a branch and is withered; and they gather them and throw them into the fire, and they are burned. If you abide in Me, and My words abide in you, you will ask what you desire, and it shall be done for you. By this My Father is glorified, that you bear much fruit; so you will be My disciples.

It is impossible to have the kind of marriage that God has intended for us without being filled with His Holy Spirit. In order to be truly filled with His Spirit, we are going to have to submit to the pruning process. The secret of the successful Christian life and marriage is to learn to abide in Jesus Christ. The fruit of the Spirit and the blessings that come from living a Spirit-filled life come naturally when we are abiding in Christ.

However, there will be seasons in our Christian life when God as the heavenly Vinedresser is going to cut back and prune those areas in our lives that need pruning so that greater fruitfulness can come about. For Kristina and I there were subtle attitudes of self-reliance, a resistance to the Spirit of God and a hardness of heart that God was going to deal with. Also, both Kristina and myself were trying to find satisfaction and completion in the entertainment business. In a sense, the film business was an idol that was erected in our hearts. God was cutting away and pruning all these things so He could produce fruitfulness.

In addition, at that time in our marriage we did not want children. Although we were not really aware of it, both of us were scarred by our painful and dysfunctional pasts. One of the things God was doing in this pruning process was getting us ready to be a father and mother and doing a deep healing work. Kristina was trying to find purpose and fulfillment as an actress, and I was trying to find meaning as a film producer. However, God, in accordance with Genesis 1:28, knew that we would only find total fulfillment when we began the journey of being fruitful and having children. God knew us better than we knew ourselves.

Over a decade later, after the Lord did a deep work of inner healing and pruning, we would discover the reality of real fruitfulness as described in Psalm 128:2–4: "…you shall be happy, and it shall be well with you. Your wife shall be like a fruitful vine in the very heart of your house, your children like olive plants all around your table. Behold, thus shall the man be who fears the LORD." Years later, after we had Paul and then our twins, Michael and Jennifer, we discovered the joyous reality of that promise. But that promise only came to fruition through the pruning process.

Below is a list of possible issues where the Lord may be pruning you to produce greater fruitfulness in your life, relationship and marriage:

1.  Cutting back all self-reliant attitudes in order to create dependence on Jesus Christ rather than self.

2.  Cutting out all idols in our hearts such as money,

career, sex and self. God gives us those things to enjoy, but they can never come before Him.

3. Pruning back wrong and sinful attitudes such as anger, bitterness, unbelief, resentment, self-will, hardness of heart, stinginess, smallness of heart, self-righteousness, rebellion and disobedience.

Instead of resenting the pruning process, look at it as God's time of preparation. He sees your potential and is preparing you to fulfill it.

# Section III
# Steps to Emotional Healing

*11*

···········································································

# Characteristics
# of Your Parents'
# Marriage

A FTER OUR WEDDING, Kristina and I moved into our
first apartment in Hoboken, New Jersey, with
suitcases literally bursting with dysfunctional programming, negative habit patterns and generational curses
that would profoundly affect our marriage. (When we
use the phrase "generational curse," we are not talking
about some kind of voodoo curse. We recognize that
this term has been misused by some. We are simply
talking about the results of sin and how they can be
transmitted from generation to generation.) The tragedy
was that nobody prepared us for what was about to
happen.

Both of us came from dysfunctional homes where

alcoholism played a major factor in the home life. My parents were divorced when I was around thirteen years old, and her parents had a noncommunicative relationship that had serious problems. As such, seemingly normal things like healthy communication, conflict resolution, love, a positive self-image, emotional nurturing, bonding with parents and healthy roles for the husband and wife were basically non-existent. It is said that adult children of alcoholics don't know what normal is. That was certainly true in our case.

Here is a description of some of the emotional baggage each of us brought into our marriage.

## PAUL'S EMOTIONAL BAGGAGE

1.  No idea of what it meant to be a positive husband
2.  Considered constant arguments and conflicts normal
3.  Suppressed anger toward father and mother
4.  Deep-rooted insecurity concerning masculinity
5.  Poor self-image
6.  Had no idea what it meant to really love or serve wife
7.  Did not know what it meant to be the leader
8.  Adult child of an alcoholic
9.  Considered anger, rage, losing temper, yelling and screaming normal
10. Emotionally abusive father

## KRISTINA'S EMOTIONAL BAGGAGE

1.  Emotionally distant from father
2.  Lack of trust and suspicious of male/authority figures
3.  Suppressed anger toward father
4.  Ignorant of healthy communication skills
5.  Had no idea of a healthy role of the wife
6.  Rejection issues
7.  Insecurity
8.  Adult child of an alcoholic
9.  Emotionally abusive father
10. Fear issues

We are not trying to blame all of our problems on our past. It is simply that the lack of healing over unresolved issues and the lack of marriage training basically guaranteed disaster.

The problem is that today many people are now coming from dysfunctional and divorced homes, and marriage skills simply do not come automatically. I realize it is very trendy to use the word *dysfunctional*. However, whether you use a trendy word or not, it's a fact that the kind of marriage your parents had is going to have a great deal of effect on your marriage.

A word of caution: No marriage is perfect. Every marriage is going to experience negative qualities, and there will be seasons when these negative aspects seem to increase. However, if your early childhood environment was one where these negative characteristics were the rule year after year, then it would be an honest appraisal of your childhood environment and your parents' marriage to say it was dysfunctional. We are not victims of our past, but we are influenced by our past. It is important to understand the environment that helped to shape and mold us so that we can trust God to find healing for our present.

Forgiveness is a key aspect of inner healing. Forgiveness will break the chains to our past. With God's help we can become overcomers and live victoriously in our marriages and families. But we need to understand something about our early conditioning so that the strongholds that may have been erected in our minds can be dismantled.

Below are two lists that reflect a positive and healthy marriage as well as a negative and unhealthy one. Review the list and see how many of these attributes reflect your parents' marriage as well as your home life. Again, no marriage is perfect, and even the best of marriages have negative components. The question is, What was the predominant atmosphere in your family's lives season after season?

| THE DYSFUNCTIONAL MARRIAGE | THE HEALTHY MARRIAGE |
| --- | --- |
| Negativity | Optimism |
| Hatred | Love |
| Arguing | Communicating |
| Bitterness | Forgiveness |
| Addiction | Sobriety |

| THE DYSFUNCTIONAL MARRIAGE | THE HEALTHY MARRIAGE |
|---|---|
| Sexual dysfunctions | Whole sexuality |
| Resentment | Empowerment |
| Cursing | Blessing |
| Put downs | Lifting up |
| Insults | Praise |
| Depression | Joy |
| Self-pity | Thankfulness |
| Confusion | Peace |
| Fighting | Discussing |
| Emotional distancing | Emotional closeness |
| Feeling left out | Feeling included |
| Rejection | Acceptance |
| Fear | Faith |
| Poverty consciousness (even if wealthy characterized by clutching of material possessions and money) | Trusting God for provisions (even if poor) |
| Husband and wife distant | Husband and wife romancing |
| Husband and wife showing no outward signs of affection | Husband and wife showing outward signs of affection |
| Husband and wife never telling each other "I love you" | Husband and wife telling each other "I love you" |
| Criticism | Encouragement |
| Awkward silence | Laughter |
| Anxiety | Fun |

Clearly, no home environment is going to be exclusively positive or negative. But if the overwhelming emotional tone of the family and parents' marriage was negative and dysfunctional, then the child learned to model this behavior at an early age. A certain degree of stronghold or negative programming has been built up in the human personality, which must be undone before this child can experience marital fulfillment and blessing.

What often happens is that people who accept Jesus Christ after coming from a negative past get married and forget about their past. For a time everything seems to go OK, but when the pressures or conflicts arise, this early childhood programming surfaces and interferes with their present marriage relationship. Even if a husband or wife has forgiven his or her parents and released them, there can still be the residue of painful past experiences affecting the person's personalities.

The key is not to get lost in some kind of endless maze regarding your past pain or to spend unnecessary time digging up past hurts. God has called us to live in the present—not the past. However, there are times when the Holy Spirit will reveal to us a stronghold in our past that is affecting our present, and this stronghold needs to be dismantled by the power of God's Word.

We must always remember that God is busy at work in us through the power of the Holy Spirit, rebuilding us and strengthening us. He is taking us to a promised land of blessing, purpose and fulfillment. Yet sometimes there are giants in that promised land that must be slain before we can possess it.

God's goal for us is marital wholeness and blessing. He will renew our minds with His Word, and as we open up our lives and trust in Him, He will bring about inner healing. Our focus should never be on our past, our hurt or our pain. Our focus must be on Jesus Christ. As we worship Him and exalt Him in our lives, if He chooses to reveal something about our past, then we must cooperate with the Holy Spirit in allowing Him to dismantle a stronghold. But our attention, worship and praise must be fixed on Him and His abundant resources—never on our lack or our pain. As we fix our eyes on Jesus, then and only then will our lives be transformed.

........................................

# 12

# Step 1: Consult the Great Psychiatrist

M Y WIFE AND I would not be married today if we did not go to God for emotional healing from our pasts. No amount of Christian marriage encounters or Christian group therapy can substitute for the firsthand healing power of the Great Psychiatrist. It was God who built our minds in the first place. He put the wiring together with all the neurons. God designed us as emotional beings. So God knows how to take us apart, cleanse and restore us. In the following chapters my wife, Kristina, will give her testimony and teach on the steps to emotional healing.

Kristina writes: On June 4, 1972, I accepted Jesus into my life. I had no one praying for me, yet I woke up one day and wanted to go to church. It was a Baptist church.

I don't think anyone had been saved in it for twenty years. When the pastor gave an altar call, I went up. That was a moment that was burned into me like a flaming torch. Nothing was the same after that.

However, I had one huge flaw that I didn't become aware of until several years later. It was that I had a very poor authority figure (my father) when I was growing up. So when I became a Christian, it was very difficult to allow God to be my heavenly Father. I allowed Jesus to be my Savior, but I had tremendous difficulty relating to God as my Father.

One of the reasons I became an actress on television and in feature films in Hollywood for a number of years was due to my need to find some kind of "emotional home," which I lacked growing up. Acting became a second home for me. In acting, I found a substitute for fatherly acceptance. It was a place to work out my subconscious problems and see life through someone else's window. However, it is also a place where you don't have to grow up. You are encouraged to be childlike. Any kind of authority figure is usually considered to be stiff or the evil person in the drama. Although this is a generalization, it is true more often than not. From James Dean to Marilyn Monroe to Demi Moore to Madonna—these people are not role models for stable, God-fearing people.

Yet when I began to walk in a closer relationship to the Lord, and He became, in a sense, my Great Psychiatrist, the Holy Spirit revealed to me these strongholds that had been erected in my life due to my past. These powerful strongholds had affected my marriage, my own psychological well-being and my relationship to others.

Allow the Holy Spirit to rule your life—from your sex life to your job. Don't allow your mind to rule your life. Of course, the Holy Spirit works in partnership with your mind and your own human spirit. We are not talking about some superspiritual or mystical experience. We are simply talking about saturating your mind with the Word of God and living a life of worship and praise where you can learn to discern His voice above your fears and sometimes distorted human emotions. I have found that when I don't read the Word on a daily basis, my mind will go to fear-based consciousness where my emotions seem to be out of control.

The key to getting your emotions and feelings under control is to give them completely over to Jesus. This is not always easy to do. Below are some steps to help you:

*Be honest.* Begin by being completely honest with God in prayer. Tell Him exactly how you feel. Open yourself up totally to God. Do not attempt to hide from God any emotion, thought or feeling, no matter how dark or ugly it may be. Hebrews 10:19–22 tells us:

> Therefore, brethren, having boldness to enter the Holiest by the blood of Jesus, by a new and living way which He consecrated for us, through the veil, that is, His flesh, and having a High Priest over the house of God, let us draw near with a true heart in full assurance of faith, having our hearts sprinkled from an evil conscience and our bodies washed with pure water.

*Be specific.* Be specific to God about how you really feel. If you are resentful, angry or mad, tell God. Talk to God about any situation or incident on your heart.

*Praise Jesus.* No matter what your feelings are, begin to praise and worship Him aloud. As images of pain and conflict enter your mind, decide as an act of your will to praise God. It may be helpful to play worship and praise music in your car or house. Psalm 146:1–2 tells us:

> Praise the LORD! Praise the LORD, O my soul! While I live, I will praise the LORD; I will sing praises to my God while I have my being.

*Cleanse your heart.* Ask God to cleanse you of any wrong attitudes or thoughts of bitterness, anger, resentment, self-centeredness and so forth. Ask Him to renew a right spirit in you.

> Behold, You desire truth in the inward parts, and in the hidden part You will make me to know wisdom. Purge me with hyssop, and I shall be clean; wash me, and I shall be whiter than snow. Make me hear joy and gladness, that the bones You have broken may rejoice. Hide Your face from my sins, and blot out all my iniquities. Create in me a clean heart, O God, and renew a steadfast spirit within me. Do not cast me away from Your presence, and do not take Your Holy Spirit from me.
>
> —PSALM 51:6–11

If we say that we have no sin, we deceive ourselves, and the truth is not in us. If we confess our sins, He is faithful and just to forgive us our sins and to cleanse us from all unrighteousness. If we say that we have not sinned, we make Him a liar, and His word is not in us.

—1 JOHN 1:8–10

*Ask God to change you.* Ask God to heal, change and transform the situation. Begin by asking Him to change you, and then pray for the other person. Jesus said, "If you ask anything in My name, I will do it" (John 14:14).

*Speak the Word.* Speak the Word of God into the situation, and claim the promises of God.

For assuredly, I say to you, whoever says to this mountain, "Be removed and be cast into the sea," and does not doubt in his heart, but believes that those things he says will be done, he will have whatever he says. Therefore I say to you, whatever things you ask when you pray, believe that you receive them, and you will have them.

—MARK 11:23–24

# 13

# Step 2:
# Begin by
# Forgiving

IF YOUR SPOUSE was raised in an environment where he or she did not receive love from the parents, your spouse will probably be critical and hard to live with.

People who were emotionally wounded in their past often will bring those unresolved issues into their present-day marriage and personal relationships. One thing that keeps people bound to their past problems is unforgiveness toward those who have hurt or wounded them.

In my own life, the Holy Spirit as God's Psychiatrist revealed to me that I had a tremendous amount of unforgiveness toward my father and mother, which was affecting my present-day relationship with my husband. I was raised in a middle-upper-class neighborhood. We had a nice home. However, our life at home was extremely dysfunctional. My father was emotionally distant and was often emotionally abusive. To compound the problem, there were sexual addictions and alcoholism in my family. As I uncovered some family secrets, I began to understand the reasons for the emotional coldness and abuse.

As early as the age of nine years, I discovered that my father was having an affair. In fact, both of my parents were having affairs. Years later I discovered that my father had almost a second family and that he was having a relationship with another woman for years. Maybe this explains why he was so distant and cold to me, especially when I became a Christian in 1972. I really believe that my parents would have preferred that I became anything but a Christian. You see, my parents represent the way many middle-class families live today who do not have a personal relationship with Jesus Christ.

Pornography, alcohol abuse and affairs are all too common behind the neatly manicured lawns and homes of "Pleasant Valley Sunday" middle-class America. Beneath the pleasant smiles and superficial hellos lies an open grave of spiritual death.

## Dysfunctional Pasts

All of us have had negative childhood experiences that can profoundly affect our marriage relationships. But when your past is one negative experience after another, then you have what psychologists call a dysfunctional past.

In my own past, there are so many negative memories. I remember when I was eleven years old, and my brother and I were watching my father's new TV. My father had told us not to watch his television and had even locked it up, but my brother picked the lock, and we watched TV for two hours. When we heard his car come in the driveway, we quickly turned off the TV, put the lock back on and got out of the room. But when he walked in, he went straight to the TV and put his hand on it. It was warm. He then confronted me and asked me where the key was. I was very stubborn and refused to tell him that my brother had picked the lock. In a rage, he dumped my clothes out of my dresser drawers, tore my room apart, grabbed his belt and started beating me. Confusion and madness were in the air. My brother then proceeded to stand up to him. A fist fight took place while my mother sat silently on the sidelines. This was our family time together.

Unfortunately, even after I became a Christian and entered marriage, I still carried this emotional baggage with me. The deep unforgiveness, rage and hostility I had toward my father was transferred to my husband. Accepting Jesus Christ into your life is not like waving a magic wand that makes your problems just disappear. I needed to release this pain to God and be healed through forgiveness toward my parents—especially my father.

Another major event to which I needed to apply forgiveness occurred when I was nineteen years old. I was on a date with a young man whom I really liked. He liked me. My father saw us driving up in front of our house. He came out into the driveway and demanded that I get out of the car. When I didn't move fast enough, he yanked me by the hair and dragged me inside my house in front of my date. Humiliation and shame overwhelmed me. I still experience the shame, even to this day. When this painful memory comes up, the only way I can get rid of the shame is to ask the Holy Spirit into the deep recesses of my mind. I ask Jesus to cover me with His blood in this memory. I ask Jesus to cleanse my heart from all anger and unforgiveness toward my father.

My prayer to God goes something like this:

> *God, I ask You to take that stronghold out of my life, that point of bondage, that point of woundedness. Let that wound be a hole where rivers of living water will come gushing out from my innermost being. Lord, I give that rock to You that is in my spirit. Holy Spirit, cleanse me from all bitterness and anger. Please forgive me for hating him and having hate so strong that I wanted to kill him. Lord, I release that hatred to You and ask You to help me to forgive him.*

Many men and women have tremendous hatred and resentment toward their parents. If these issues are not properly resolved, they will affect their marriage and other relationships in life. If children don't have healthy father figures—especially boys—when they enter into marriage, emotional problems will surface in the husband/wife relationship and the parent/child relationships. Although at first, especially in the courtship phase of the relationship, everything will seem like smooth sailing, sooner or later they will hit an emotional iceberg with massive unresolved issues like anger and resentment. It is precisely here where a lot of Christians get into trouble. In our day when many come from dysfunctional families and wounded pasts, it is simply not enough to have good intentions and get married. There are many people who read the Bible, have accepted Jesus Christ into their lives and go to church who are carrying destructive emotional baggage from their past.

It's not that every Christian couple needs to go into therapy in order to have a happy marriage. But God created us as psychological beings, and these unresolved psychological and spiritual issues need to be dealt with in order for us to experience the blessings God has intended for us in marriage and family relationships. Failure to do so invites disaster. This is why we see so many Christian marriages, even in leadership, breaking up and why we constantly hear of affairs, sexual addictions, divorce, homosexuality and abuse even in Christian lives. The reason for this is that although these people are saved, the Lord has not been allowed to penetrate the deep recesses of their hearts and minds. There are still unresolved issues and secret compartments in their souls that have yet to be exposed to the light.

## FORGIVENESS AND FAMILY SECRETS

One of the attributes of a marriage or family that is dysfunctional or in spiritual darkness is that there are hidden secrets. Affairs, addictions, secret sins, molestation, homosexuality and other sins are kept secret. Even though they are kept secret, they still have devastating effects on marriages and families. These "works of darkness" cause spiritual, physical and psychological problems.

In my own personal journey toward wholeness, I had to confront the reality that my father was living a double life and that for many years he maintained a mistress.

I was not a Christian when I was in high school, and I was a rebellious teenager. My friends and I decided to take my dad's car while he was at work. We knew he parked it outside a house about two miles from work and walked to work from there. So we took the car for a few hours and then parked it back in front of the house. What puzzled me was that when he got home from work, he knew that I had taken the car. It was only many years later, after his death, that I figured out how he knew I took the car. Shortly after he died, it was discovered that he had a mistress who lived in that house where he parked the car. My father always said he was going to eat breakfast with his friend. Now I know that the reason he never ate breakfast at home with us was that he had another family. Needless to say, this revelation devastated my mother.

If you discover "works of darkness" that were hidden in your family, be sure to go to your heavenly Father for healing so that those secrets will not cause more problems in your life.

## STEPS TO UNCOVER FAMILY SECRETS
## AND WORKS OF DARKNESS

### Step 1: Acknowledge the truth (Ps. 90:8).

Begin by admitting what really happened. Do not suppress or deny the truth.

1.  Were you emotionally or sexually abused as a child?

2.  Were either of your parents an alcoholic or addicted to drugs, legal or illegal?

3.  Was there hidden sexual addiction in your family? Was your father secretly watching pornography in magazines, videos or films?

4.  Did either of your parents have an affair?

5.  What secrets were hidden or covered by your family?

6.  What areas of shame were kept covered in your family?

### Step 2: Present the secret works of darkness to the Lord.

Recognize that in Jesus Christ you are no longer a victim. Do not sweep the truth under the carpet or suppress it. Understand that your life is in God's sovereign plan. Take up your role as an intercessor. "And we know that all things work together for good to those who love God, to those who are the called according to His purpose" (Rom. 8:28).

### *Step 3: Engage in the warfare of worship.*

1.  Name specifically each work of darkness and family secret before the Lord in prayer.

2.  As an intercessor, ask God to cleanse the individuals, yourself and the situation with His blood (1 John 1:7–10). It is true that the individuals involved are responsible to God for their own repentance. But you are acting as an intercessor in dismantling the works of darkness.

3.  As the shameful images and memories come up, praise and worship God. You are not praising Him for the acts of sin, but you are worshiping Him in the midst of it.

4.  As you open up and release your past to the Lord, you are releasing His power to set you free and redeem your past.

### PARTNERS IN DARKNESS

Walk in the Spirit, and you shall not fulfill the lust of the flesh. For the flesh lusts against the Spirit, and the Spirit against the flesh; and these are contrary to one another, so that you do not do the things that you wish.... Now the works of the flesh are evident, which are: adultery, fornication, uncleaness, lewdness...

—GALATIANS 5:16–17, 19

The subject of affairs, lying and sexual immorality seem to dominate our news media and film industry. The affairs of the president of the United States, the lies and cover-ups are the subject of our television talk shows. In addition, we witness the silence of the First Lady, who does not comment about the president's many affairs. Also, the affairs of our senators and congressmen are leaked to the press for international exposure. However, beneath all these affairs and sexual immorality are often untold devastating effects on spouses and children. Even if an affair remains hidden, it always produces destructive consequences in the marriages and families.

Children are especially wounded by the unfaithfulness of their parents, even if this is never brought out in the open. A child experiences the emotional devastation of a parent's adulterous relationship. In a very real sense, the person having an affair becomes emotionally disconnected from the family. Adultery produces a spiritual and emotional death in a family. Children sense the emotional distance of parents whose actions of love and caring are being committed outside of the home. They become deeply wounded, which brings about depression, anger, rebellion, sexual immorality and other problems.

Children act out this inner pain in many forms of rebellion. They are screaming for answers and not getting them. They are screaming for a loving father and not getting him. They come home only to find a morgue-type atmosphere. A child may feel guilty and think he was the cause for the death in the marriage. A horrible sense of inner shame and insecurity develops that begins to warp the child's character. Children are too young to understand that there is a web of deceit being spun all around them that is choking the life out of them.

Adults suffer from affairs, also. At first they think they are getting away with it. But then the repressed emotions start to surface on their own. Depression, anger and guilt poison the soul like a deep wound or infection that has set in. When the God of the universe created men and women, He knew full well their spiritual, emotional and sexual nature. This is why God gave us commandments against adultery, sexual immorality and lying. God is not being a "party pooper." God's purpose was to protect men, women and children from the horrible destruction that unfaithfulness always brings.

## FORGIVENESS, THE KEY TO RELEASE

Here are some key steps to take if you have been wounded by affairs in your childhood home or your adult life.

First, in any marriage it is vitally important for us to diligently guard our hearts against the temptation to be unfaithful either physically or even mentally. We live in a society that actually encourages unfaithfulness, and we need to be watchful over our thoughts and emotions. Affairs don't just happen. They begin with small compromises and emotional bonding with members of the opposite sex.

Second, unfaithfulness or adultery must be dealt with in

a marriage. It cannot be just swept under the carpet or overlooked. There must be true repentance and a complete turning away from sin. Pastoral counseling should be involved in order for complete reconciliation in a marriage to occur.

Forgive the people or person who has wounded you. Many of us have been deeply wounded by a parent's or spouse's adultery. There has been very real emotional hurt and woundedness that can take a lifetime to overcome. My father's and mother's affairs deeply wounded me as a child because they produced a death of love and intimacy in our family. The result was rejection, anger, shame and many other negative things that became part of our lives.

Forgiveness is the key to deliverance and healing. As long as we harbor resentment, hatred, bitterness and anger in our hearts, we will be kept a prisoner to the very things we seek to escape. We are not talking about a glib or superficial kind of "I forgive you." We are talking about allowing the Great Psychiatrist, who is the Holy Spirit, to go into the deep recesses of our mind, heart, memories and emotions and to release that pain and hurt into His hands. Biblical forgiveness can only be produced by the work of the Holy Spirit in our lives.

Sometimes the pain and hurt are so deep that we have buried them beneath the surface of our souls as a kind of protection. Perhaps we don't want to bring them to the surface because we cannot bear the thought of once again experiencing the hideous pain, shame and hurt.

The faces, smells, sounds and experiences may surface

in our dreams or nightmares or momentarily invade our consciousness as events or people in our daily lives trigger our memories. Many times when people accidentally press our emotional "hot buttons," they have stumbled into childhood areas of pain that produce a strong and seemingly irrational reaction in us.

But if we invite Him, the Holy Spirit can go into the depths of our being and set us free from the horror and anguish that lie beneath our soul. The key is that we must willfully choose to invite Jesus Christ into those areas, and we must willfully choose to forgive by His power those who have hurt us. This is not always easy, and it may involve a long-term battle where we are continually bringing persons and events before the Lord, asking for cleansing of bitterness, hurt, rejection and unforgiveness. These prayers may go on for many years until the inner wound is finally cleansed and lasting healing and deliverance occurs.

## WARNING SIGNS OF WOUNDEDNESS

When a person or situation pushes an emotional "hot button" in your life, that is often a sign that you need to identify an unresolved issue and bring it to the Lord. My feelings of unforgiveness toward my father were brought out by a situation at my job. Due to some unfair hiring practices, I learned that I would instantly lose my seniority and be replaced by someone brand-new on the job. I went off the deep end emotionally, and I couldn't understand it because other things would not seem to bother me. I was so stressed out that Paul and I decided to drive to a Friday night service at a church about an hour from our house for some spiritual refreshment.

After the guest speaker spoke, I decided to go for prayer at the end of the service where volunteers from the church would pray for the needs of the people. A man in his late thirties asked me what my prayer needs were. After I shared my struggle at work, I expected him to start praying. Instead, out of the blue he asked me about my relationship with my father. Did I know that "Daddy God" loved, valued and accepted me just as I was?

I was somewhat shocked to hear him talk about these issues. After all, this volunteer knew nothing about my life. This was a demonstration of the Holy Spirit at work as the Great Psychiatrist. A psychologist or professional counselor may have taken many months or years to get at the heart of this core issue in my life. But here, in just a few seconds, the Holy Spirit moving through a prayer volunteer began to deal with the deep issues of my life.

Underneath all the feelings of fear and valuelessness was a deeper core issue of unforgiveness toward my father. The lack of a father's love caused me to feel unworthy and unloved at the core of my being. My unforgiveness toward my father allowed me to stay in the place of feeling valueless, which amplified my problem at work. Because I never felt accepted and loved by my father, I attempted to win this approval through performance.

The prayer volunteer reminded me of the parable in Matthew 18:23–35 where an unforgiving servant who had been forgiven by his master then refused to forgive those who came to him asking for forgiveness. In verses 18:34–35 Jesus said, "And his master was angry, and delivered him to the torturers until he should be all that was due him. So My heavenly Father also will do to you if each of you, from his heart, does not forgive his brother his trespasses."

This parable from Jesus teaches us that it is we who will be imprisoned and in emotional bondage if we do not forgive the people who have abused us in our lives. Because Jesus had forgiven all my sins when I invited Jesus Christ into my life, I was required by God to forgive all those who had sinned against me, including my father. If I did not truly forgive my father then, as Jesus said in the parable, I would be "delivered to the torturers" or "tormenters." This is a very heavy spiritual principle!

Below is a prayer you can use as a starting point for forgiveness and healing in your own life.

## A PRAYER FOR FORGIVENESS

*Jesus Christ, I come to You right now and open myself up before You. God, I confess that I have unforgiveness against _____. Lord, I bring before You these memories and experiences.* [Write down and name the painful memories and experiences before the Lord. Then place the list in your hand and pray with your hand open, signifying that you are giving up these things to the Lord.] *Lord, I give over to You right now the pain, hurt, woundedness, anger, bitterness and rejection I experienced.*

*Lord, what _____ did was wrong. But Father, in Jesus' name, I choose to forgive _____ right now. By the power of Your Holy Spirit I release _____ to You. Lord, I also ask You to forgive me for holding unforgiveness against _____. Cleanse my heart, Lord, right now by Your blood, and deliver me now by Your power. Lord, Your Word says that we are to forgive those who have sinned against us so that we may be forgiven (Matt. 6:12). Lord, by Your power and in obedience to Your Word, I choose to forgive _____. I do this as an act of obedience and faith, Lord, not on the basis of how I feel, but because You, Jesus Christ, have commanded me to forgive. In Jesus' name, I release this to You now, and I praise and worship You. In Jesus' name, amen.*

# 14

## Step 3: Obedience to God's Word

O NE OF THE most powerful ways we can experience healing in our lives is to obey God's Word. Many people walk in subtle forms of self-deception, and they rationalize and justify disobeying God's Word and His life-giving principles. Justification, rationalization, excuses and just plain old disobedience always bring emotional bondage.

The prophet Samuel said, "Behold, to obey is better than sacrifice...for rebellion is as the sin of witchcraft" (1 Sam. 15:22–23).

When I became a Christian, I thought that being obedient meant going to church three times a week. But what I found out after twenty years is that I had an intense desire to please people before pleasing God. I had to be liked, or I could not function.

Many times depression, anxiety, fear, self-pity and unhappiness stem from disobedience to God's principles. No amount of therapy, counseling or medication can alleviate suffering that is brought on by disobedience to God's Word. Each of us must keep watch over our own hearts and lives, because through the Fall of Man each one of us has an ever-present capacity to deceive ourselves. Here are some general principles that can help us to be obedient to the Lord.

### 1. Don't be a people pleaser.

If you are trying to earn people's acceptance rather than God's, you are going to get into trouble. People with low self-esteem are especially vulnerable in this area.

Many people are not really being themselves. They fear rejection, and so they put on an act in order to be accepted. It is important to understand that the root of this problem is the fear of rejection. Some people are so convinced that if they really exposed themselves, they would not be liked. This is a powerful stronghold that was created by being emotionally rejected by one or both parents. God wants to move into this area of your personality and remove this deep-rooted fear of rejection. He can do this when you forgive the parent who rejected you and open yourself up to the love of God. Many people who call themselves Christians have never really experienced being totally accepted, forgiven and loved by God the Father. Although they understand this intellectually, they never have experienced it and felt it on a deep emotional and spiritual level. It is possible for you to experience just how much God loves and values you.

### 2. Don't follow the world.

The values, belief systems and morals that come at us from the media, our neighbors and coworkers on the job are often in direct opposition to God's values and priorities. The Bible states, "Do not be conformed to this world, but be transformed by the renewing of your mind" (Rom. 12:2). Our attitudes toward marriage, sex, family, fashion and career should be shaped by biblical values and not by the ideas presented in the media and popular culture. This does not mean we have to look and dress like monks in a monastery. It simply means our values should be based on God's values.

### 3. Fast and pray.

Regular fasting and prayer can break bonds of wickedness in the invisible realm. We do not impress God with our going hungry. However, fasting done with the right spirit releases tremendous kingdom power on any situation.

### 4. Get rid of occult or pornographic material.

Get rid of any materials in your home or life that involve the New Age, astrology, meditation, the occult or false religions. Music, books, jewelry and other things that are occultic can allow spiritual oppression to remain in your life.

Also, any form of pornography in the form of videos, magazines, cable television and even the Internet must be removed from your home. Tragically, married couples today who are ignorant of God's ways or have become disobedient think it's OK to watch X-rated videos. Pornography in any form allows a spirit of lust and perversion into the home, which will always have devastating effects.

### 5. Understand what God requires by reading His Word.

Read the Bible on a daily or regular basis.

### 6. Submit to a local Bible-believing church.

A husband and wife and any children should be committed members of a local Bible-believing church and accountable to members of that congregation. A spiritual covering exists over the marriage and home of a husband and wife who belong to and attend a local Bible-believing church. This protective covering is removed when the husband and wife are not a committed part of a local body, and this makes them vulnerable to spiritual attacks against their marriage and home.

### 7. Have fellowship with other believers in Jesus Christ.

Be very careful about developing friendships with nonbelievers. Nonbelievers will always bring worldly advice into your life. A married couple needs to have relationships with mature, Bible-believing Christians who can bring a positive spiritual influence into their lives.

Some churches have home group meetings or cell groups that can be very beneficial.

## 8. Tithe, because your finances are tied into your heart.

One of the greatest stress points in a marriage is in the area of finances. Financial pressure can bring stress and tension into a marriage as no other force can. However, if God's people would obey the Lord in the area of tithes and finances, they would discover that God would bless them financially.

When Pastor Jack Hayford was a guest on Paul's radio show, "Home Builders," the theme of the day was "How to Get Hell Out of the Home." Pastor Hayford spoke about the need for married couples to be obedient in the area of their tithes and offerings. Malachi 3:8–11 says:

> "Will a man rob God? Yet you have robbed Me! But you say, 'In what way have we robbed You?' In tithes and offerings. You are cursed with a curse, for you have robbed me, even this whole nation. Bring all the tithes into the storehouse, that there may be food in My house, and try Me now in this," says the Lord of hosts, "if I will not open for you the windows of heaven and pour out for you such blessing that there will not be room enough to receive it. And I will rebuke the devourer for your sakes, so that he will not destroy the fruit of your ground, nor shall the vine fail to bear fruit for you in the field," says the LORD of hosts.

## A PRAYER OF OBEDIENCE

These eight steps are crucial for the survival of your marriage. You can use the following prayer to ask the Lord to help you walk in obedience on a daily basis.

*Lord Jesus Christ, I come to You today, and as an act of my will I choose to surrender to You in every area of my life. God, I ask You to reveal to me any area where I am in disobedience.* [Spend a few moments waiting on the Lord and allowing Him to reveal anything in your life that is displeasing to Him. Write down the areas of disobedience.]

_____.

*Jesus, I ask You to forgive me for disobeying You in the above areas of my life. I ask You to cleanse me with Your blood. Jesus Christ, give me an obedient spirit.* [It may be helpful at this point in your prayer to lie face down on the floor or carpet before the Lord. Hold nothing back from Him.] *Jesus, forgive me for my self-centeredness. I ask You to make me completely Yours. I ask that You would consume me with Your presence. I ask that You would forgive me of rebellion. I renounce* [name specific things or activities that you know are sinful] _____.

*Jesus Christ, I ask that You would be Lord of my life. I yield myself to Your will, and I ask that You take complete control of my life. Jesus, You are my Lord and Master. I give You my entire life. I give You my husband (or wife)* [name them] _____, *and I give You my child(ren)* [give their names] _____. *I lift my family up to You in prayer, asking that You move into our lives and take full control. I thank You for doing this, in Jesus' name.*

*Lord, as an act of obedience to Your Word, I give You 10 percent of my income as a tithe to You. In Jesus' name, amen.*

*15*

---

# Step 4: Seek Deliverance From the Root of Oppression

ELIVERANCE REMOVES PAST brokenness and bondage so the real you can come forth. It is important to understand that we are talking about the Holy Spirit's ability to sever bondages in a person's life. A believer in Jesus Christ cannot be possessed by an evil spirit, but a believer can be oppressed externally and influenced by spirits. For example, addiction to alcohol or pornography is a psychological mechanism that is used to cover up pain. However, these psychological mechanisms are often rooted in a generational curse. Therefore, a believer in Jesus Christ who is addicted to alcohol or pornography may be influenced by a generational curse of alcoholism or sexual immorality where very real demonic oppression is at work. A distinct delivering work by the Holy Spirit is needed for that person to be set free.

Christians can and do experience spiritual oppression. This oppression can come from demonic activity in the invisible realm where a door has been opened spiritually. Residue from the past or the need for deep inner healing in the present can provide a gateway for demonic oppression. For example, Christians who harbor unforgiveness, rejection, anger or bitterness in their hearts can open the door to Satan's control in their lives if these issues are not properly dealt with. Spirits of lust, addiction, fear, depression, poverty, sickness, anger and confusion, among others, can adversely influence a person's life.

Many times when a Christian is disobedient to the Lord, these bondages can attach themselves to their lives. For example, a Christian who chooses to disobey the Lord and watch X-rated videos or pictures on the Internet can open himself up to a spirit of lust.

## HAVE YOU TAKEN YOUR GARBAGE OUT LATELY?

One of the things that the Holy Spirit does in all of our lives is "spiritual house cleaning." As we walk with the Lord on a daily basis, He will illuminate certain areas of our lives that He wants to deal with. When He convicts us of a sin, habit pattern, thought process or action that He wants us to get rid of, we have a choice whether to obey or disobey. In short, He wants us to take out our spiritual garbage so He can clean our inner houses!

In my own life, I have a real problem in the area of trusting God with my children's futures and yielding to a spirit of fear. The Holy Spirit has convicted me of thought patterns, meditations and beliefs that all originate from the generational curse of fear that was deposited in my life through my parents. However, I cannot blame my parents for my disobedience to the Lord in this area. The Word of God continually commands us to trust in the Lord and to have faith in Him and His Word. When I meditate, think about and worry about my children, I have chosen to disobey God and to sin in the area of my thought life. It is my disobedience to God's command to trust and believe Him that is allowing a spirit of fear to bring bondage into my own life.

I have to be honest and transparent before God and come before Him and admit that I have a real problem trusting my children's futures to Him. The problems start when I see the wasteland of humanity all around me, and I worry about my children becoming part of that wasteland. In this thought process I think I am being "realistic" and that as a Christian parent I should take every step I can to raise my children in the ways of the Lord and to protect them from the snares of the evil one.

Yet if I am truly being "realistic," according to God's definition, then I must incorporate into my thinking process the truths of His Word. I must not give in to a spirit of fear, which ends up emotionally draining me and actually causing the things I fear most, because a parent bound by fear cannot pass on faith to his or her children.

Instead I must choose to think in line with the Word of God and allow the Holy Spirit to dismantle these fear-based strongholds in my life. I must understand that the enemy will use legitimate parental concern and twist it into a oppressive fear and paranoia that can rob our souls of everything that God has for us.

This does not meant that we simply "throw caution to the wind" or glibly say "I am just trusting the Lord," as so many do. What they really mean is, "I have chosen to be irresponsible and neglect my God-given assignment to be steward over my children's lives." No, it means that I must continue to be a diligent Christian parent who is involved in my children's lives. But after I have been diligent and done what I can, I must intercede for my children and entrust them to the Lord's care and protection.

## UNDERSTANDING THE
## ROOT CAUSE OF OPPRESSION

When we allow the Holy Spirit to be our Great Psy-chiatrist, we can uncover the root cause of our spiritual bondage or oppression. It's not that we want to wallow in our past or spend an excessive amount of time rehearsing our hurts, but sometimes it is important to understand the source of our bondage. For example, it is possible to inherit spiritual bondage from our parents. Numbers 14:18 talks about visiting the iniquity of the fathers on the children to the third and fourth generation.

You may not know what your ancestors were up to, but you may have an idea what your parents were up to. My mother had regular card readings and went to fortune-tellers. She had books in her house by psychic Edgar Cayce (1877–1945) and wanted anything "spiritual" except the biblical Jesus. As such, a very real spiritual oppression existed in my childhood, and I do not want this generational curse of the occult to be passed on to my children. Therefore, I have drawn a spiritual line in the sand with the blood of Jesus Christ. Through fasting, prayer, intercession and specific prayers against these generational curses, I have bound the activity of the enemy through the power of the prayer of agreement with my husband.

We need to recognize the things that open up the door for spiritual oppression in our marriages and families. Some of these doorways can be the following:

- Lying and not confessing the lies as a sin before God
- Occult practices
- Tragedy resulting in unresolved pain
- Long-term negative emotions that have erected strongholds in our minds
- Continual hardening of your heart toward God

## THE PRESENCE OF GOD

In dealing with deliverance it is important to understand that God has not left us as victims or orphans in life. God has made available to all of us supernatural power that can break these bondages and lead us into healing and freedom. When I was still an actress in New

York City, the Lord led me to a place where I could experience this supernatural power.

Many Christians are afraid of opening themselves up to the supernatural power of God. Subconsciously they attempt to regulate or control their relationship with God. As believers in Jesus Christ, we must never be afraid of opening ourselves up at the deepest dimensions to the presence of God. When I was dating my future husband, Paul, in New York City, we visited a church on the East Side of Manhattan called Rock Church. I remember kneeling down in prayer and experiencing an overwhelming sense of the presence of God. The words of Jesus in John 7:38 came true for me: "He who believes in Me, as the Scripture has said, out of his heart will flow rivers of living water." From that moment on, I slowly began to identify strongholds in my life and could then turn to God for help.

I used to have one recurring dream. It was of a ship that was in murky waters, with only one light on. I believe that ship represented my soul. I told Paul about this dream and asked him to pray that the Holy Spirit would go into every room on that ship and turn on the lights. How much of my soul is transformed by the power of God? The choice is up to me. Forgiveness is the key to such deliverance.

Below is a prayer that you can use as an example for helping others pray for deliverance. You can also change the wording slightly and use it to go to God for your own needs as well.

## A PRAYER FOR DELIVERANCE

*Lord, we come to You this day in the name of Jesus Christ, praising Your holy name. We worship You, God, and thank You that nothing is impossible with You. Father, in the name of Jesus Christ, we ask that You would deliver _____ from _____ and anything that would not please You. Lord, we ask in the name of Jesus Christ that You would go to the root cause of this bondage and set _____ free from any strongholds, spiritual oppression and psychological mechanisms that would bind _____ to this addiction, habit or spirit.*

*In the mighty name of Jesus Christ we thank You that the weapons of our warfare are mighty through God to the pulling down of these strongholds, and in the name of Jesus we cast down any thought process, mental image, fantasy, belief system or habit of thinking that exalts itself against the knowledge of God. Father, we bring every thought under the lordship of Jesus Christ. Jesus Christ, we praise You right now that Your delivering power is at work and that You are setting _____ free. We thank You that we are washed in the blood of Jesus Christ and that there is no condemnation for those who are in Christ Jesus. We thank You that You forgive us and accept us completely if we are willing to confess our sins before You. In Jesus' name, amen.*

..........................................................................................................

# 16

# Step 5: Take Action Against Strongholds

T HE PROCESS OF dismantling strongholds can be understood by the following outline. However, first a word of caution: My purpose in discussing strongholds is not to generate an excessive or unhealthy sense of morbid introspection or to get people to go off on a tangent searching for strongholds. However, it is important to understand that some of the issues affecting our marriages are rooted in the past. It is these strongholds that need to be dealt with.

As a child I was raised on television programs like *The Twilight Zone, Outer Limits* and *Alfred Hitchcock.* What word do you think of when you meditate on these programs? The word that comes to me is *fear.* I believe that a stronghold of fear was erected in my life from watching these TV programs. Maybe you watched other television programs or movies that erected fear or other strongholds in your life. Perhaps you had exposure to the occult, pornography or some other thing that deposited spiritual bondage in your life. Here are some practical spiritual principles that can help you stand strong and take the promised land in your life.

### 1. Identify

Pray and ask the Holy Spirit to reveal to you if any current destructive behavior pattern is rooted in the past. Clearly identify the stronghold in your mind and how it affects your present behavior. Search your heart to see if the stronghold is tied to an issue of unforgiveness.

### 2. Confess

We give place to the powers of darkness when we have unconfessed sin in our lives. We must keep our lives totally cleansed before the Lord so as not to block God's powerful deliverance. For example, in order for me to be delivered from the stronghold of fear that watching these childhood television programs established in my life, I had to specifically renounce the entrance point where this fear was established in my life. My prayer went something like this:

> *Lord, I confess my sin of watching hour after hour of fearful television shows. Lord, I give that sin to You and ask You to cleanse me of it. I bind that spirit of fear over my life. Lord Jesus Christ, by the power of Your Holy Spirit, I ask that You tear down all strongholds of fear in my life. In Jesus' name, amen.*

When praying prayers like this, it is important to maintain theological balance. We are not talking about looking for a demon under every dinner plate or going on wild-goose chases looking for all kinds of spirits. I prayed this prayer only after the Lord revealed to me that some of my fearful thought habits were based on the fear that came into my life through watching certain television programs as a child. In other words, I was dealing with specific issues that God had brought up in my life.

In your life, the issue may not be fear related. You may have allowed alcoholism, addictions, lust, anxiety and other issues to develop through some act of disobedience. Ask the Lord if you need to confess a specific sin that allowed these strongholds to get a hold in your life.

### 3. Renounce

You have to take a firm stand against any bondage in your life. For example, when it comes to the issue of fear, it is important to stand on the Word of God and quote the Scripture verse that says, "For God has not given [me] a spirit of fear, but of power and of love and of a sound mind" (2 Tim. 1:7). If you believe that you are confronting an actual spirit of fear, then speak to that spirit and boldly say, "Evil spirit, I come against you in the name of Jesus. You have no dominion in my life. You are bound and cast into the sea. You will no longer have power in my life or my children's lives. I command you to be gone."

On the other hand, not everything that comes against us is an evil spirit. It may be our own weakness or thought patterns. Spiritual discernment is necessary. But at those times when our bondage is the result of demonic activity, we need to confront those spirits and demons with the spiritual authority that Jesus Christ has given us.

In order for us to take advantage of the spiritual weapons that Jesus Christ has given us, it is important not to be afraid to use them. For example, at our home there are times when we anoint ourselves, our children and even our physical home with oil when we pray. Sometimes we will walk through the house and worship the Lord in a loud voice and command everything that is not of Him to leave. In addition, we try to bathe our home with worship music, because Satan cannot stand the worship of God's people.

We are not trying to be "superspiritual" or superstitious. But the Bible does teach us that there is an unseen or invisible realm that affects every home, marriage and family. When we take the proper steps to do spiritual house cleaning, we are commanding evil spirits to flee, and we are inviting the presence of the Lord.

Nothing is more important than inviting the presence of the Lord into our marriages and homes. When Adam and Eve disobeyed God in the Fall, the presence of God withdrew, causing death and the unleashing of destructive forces. In our marriages and homes we can inadvertently open the door to some of these forces. This is why it is so vitally important to take the proper spiritual steps to invite God's holy presence into our lives. In His presence there is healing, fullness and joy.

### 4. Reject

Romans 12:2 says, "And do not be conformed to this world, but be transformed by the renewing of your mind, that you may prove what is that good and acceptable and perfect will of God." In our marriages we must actively reject worldly counsel and ideas that are not based on the Word of God. God may tell us to do things in our marriages and lives that go against the grain of society. We must understand what the Bible says and obey it.

### 5. Believe

Finally, we must believe that God has a special plan and purpose for each one of our lives. We must read the promises from the Bible and apply them personally to our lives, marriages and families. God did not create us to be mules, treadmill runners, slaves and victims endlessly being wearied, defeated and depressed. We must remember that we have a spiritual enemy who seeks to bring discouragement and despair, but God has a wonderful plan for your marriage and life. You must believe that and act on that fact by faith. Through the Holy Spirit, He will send you His power, which will restore and heal your life, no matter how bad things may look. Allow the Holy Spirit to paint a picture of His promised land for you and your marriage in your heart. Let Him give you a vision of what is possible, and then move out in faith and obedience to take your land.

Strongholds do not always go away instantly. Oftentimes there needs to be continual prayer over a negative habit pattern. This prayer may last years until the stronghold is fully dismantled. Remember, the powers of darkness want to see you in bondage, and there will be a contesting of the territory. Just as the Promised Land was not possessed without conflict, so you will not be able to possess freedom and release without spiritual warfare. Have faith in God's Word that He will give you the victory. Do not allow yourself to be discouraged and condemned if you find yourself failing and doing the same negative behavior. Remember, it is the mighty power of God and not your own human power that will get the job done.

# To Kristina on Her Birthday
### by Paul McGuire

*Your creative spirit*
*illuminates the grey*
*dull worlds of monotone*
  *become electric.*
*Two dimensions burst into*
  *three, four and more!*
*Flatland becomes*
*hills, valleys and mountain*
  *streams.*
*Sunrises burst into cloudy*
  *mornings, making*
*them alive.*
*Walking becomes*
*dancing;*
*love becomes*
*lovemaking;*
*dinner becomes a*
  *feast;*
*life becomes alive.*

*You are wondrous,*
*endlessly to be discovered,*
*gifts to be opened.*
*Your energy drives the day*
*and fires up the night.*
*Your spirit*
*reflects the eternal*
*when He said,*
*"Let there be light,"*
*when He filled the earth*
*with His creation.*
*You are outside*
*of time.*
*You are eternal.*
*Your love is endless,*
*your love complete.*
*In your presence*
*I find life worth living.*

# Section IV
# Sex, Romance and Avoiding Affairs

# *17*

---

# Maximum
# Sex and Love
# in Marriage

A<small>T THE VERY</small> beginning of time God established the principle of sexual, emotional and spiritual intimacy between a man and his wife. Genesis 2:24 says, "Therefore a man shall leave his father and mother and be joined to his wife, and they shall become one flesh." The phrase "one flesh" refers to sexual intercourse, child conception and emotional and spiritual oneness. God established the attraction between a man and a woman along with the whole range of sexual responses to be enjoyed within the marriage relationship.

Due to the powerful and sacred nature of sexual intercourse, sexual expression was designed by God to be exclusively experienced within the marriage relationship between a husband and a wife. Proverbs 5:18–19, which is part of a passage warning against immorality, states, "Let your fountain be blessed, and rejoice with the wife of your youth. As a loving deer and a graceful doe, let her breasts satisfy you at all times; and always be enraptured with her love."

Although this passage is directed toward men, the principle could apply to women as well. God is saying that the sexual relationship between a husband and wife is a good and holy thing. God is encouraging both men and women to enjoy fully a rich and satisfying sexual relationship. Somehow in the Christian culture, we have gotten on the defensive regarding sexuality, forgetting that it was God who created sex in the first place.

## LET THE MARRIAGE BED BE UNDEFILED

In speaking of God's affirmation of the beauty of sexuality between a husband and wife, it is important to add some clarification at this point. Hebrews 13:4 states, "Marriage is honorable among all, and the bed undefiled; but fornicators and adulterers God will judge." Clearly, God is against all sex outside of marriage and warns against people who break their marriage vows and have sexual relations with people other than their spouses. However, the marriage bed being undefiled deals with other issues also.

In our society, the basic belief regarding human sexuality is "if it feels good, do it!" This is the opposite of biblical teaching. As Christians we are free to enjoy a rich and dynamic sexual life with our spouses. But there are certain corrupt and debasing sexual activities that reflect the spirit of this world rather than the Holy Spirit. There are many sexual activities and practices that are encouraged by secular marriage books that are not things a Christian should engage in, because they debase, degrade and grieve the Holy Spirit.

In 1 Thessalonians 4:3–5 Paul warns men, "For this is the will of God, your sanctification: that you should abstain from sexual immorality; that each of you should know how to possess his own vessel in sanctification and honor, not in passion of lust, like the Gentiles who do not know God." Men are free to enjoy sexual pleasure with their wives and to have fun sexually. But Christian men and women are not to be driven and controlled by a spirit of lust. The Bible makes a distinction between the sexual drive God created and sexual perversion and lust.

In our contemporary society, a spirit of lust has permeated every level of society. The degradation and perversion of God's gift of sexuality can enter a marriage if the Christian husband and wife open themselves up to the spirit of the world. The Bible does not teach what sexual positions you should use or how you are to express yourself sexually. Even though the traditional sexual position of the husband on top of the wife has been called "the missionary position" for years, nowhere in the Bible will you find a sexual position mandated.

The motivating factor in all sexual expression between a husband and wife is found in 1 Corinthians 13:1–8 where the nature of Christian love is outlined. Any practice that violates God's commandment of love should not be practiced by the Christian couple. The Bible does not teach a tidy little set of do's and don'ts in marriage. Instead, it affirms sexuality within the general guidelines of love and the voice of the Holy Spirit. There is a difference between cultural guidelines and the voice of the Holy Spirit.

As a general rule, practices that are based on a spirit of lust, degradation or perversion are a defilement of the pure and holy marriage bed of believers and should not be practiced. Again, God gives great freedom to individual Christian couples in regard to sexual expression. However, there are some practices currently promoted in secular sex and marriage manuals that are either directly forbidden by God in the Bible or that conflict with biblical values. Some of those practices that would defile a marriage bed include:

- The use of pornography or watching pornographic videos. This practice is increasingly common in our culture, but it is a debasing activity that violates the Word of God (Matt. 5:28). In addition, it is a form of mental adultery and allows a spirit of sexual perversion and lust to enter into the home.

- Any sexual expression that encourages either partner to fantasize about someone else while they are having sexual relations with their mate. Again, this is a form of mental adultery.

- Any form of sexual perversion

- Any sexual act that the Bible specifically forbids

The overriding principle regarding sexual relations for the Christian is to enjoy God's gift of sex without allowing the world's perverted views of sexuality to invade our homes. There is a world spirit regarding human sexuality that is the antithesis of what the Bible teaches. Everything from the ready availability of pornography on cable television and the local videocassette store to the sexual perversion promoted by mainstream pop stars encourage a spirit of lust and perversion. However, God has given His people a Holy Spirit who is pure and loving. Nowhere in the Bible does God minimize the value of sexual expression. The Bible very clearly affirms sexuality within marriage.

Many people call my talk show, adding a lot of unbiblical, legalistic stuff about sex in the marriage relationship. The Bible gives a man and woman a certain freedom in expressing themselves sexually. But in today's culture, with the amount of men (and women) who have been exposed to hardcore pornography, there has been an introduction of corrupting and debasing practices. In addition, many popular women's magazines advocate sexual practices that debase and degrade the sexual experience. The Bible encourages a healthy, positive and creative sex life between a husband and wife, but it warns against allowing perversion, lust and degradation into the marriage bed.

The Song of Solomon is filled with references of sensual love between a husband and wife:

> How beautiful are your feet in sandals,
> O prince's daughter!
> The curves of your thighs are like jewels,
> The work of the hands of a skillful workman.
> Your navel is a rounded goblet;
> It lacks no blended beverage.
> Your waist is a heap of wheat
> Set about with lilies.
> Your two breasts are like two fawns,
> Twins of a gazelle....
> How fair and how pleasant you are,
> O love, with your delights!
> This stature of yours is like a palm tree,
> And your breasts like its clusters.
> I said, "I will go up to the palm tree,
> I will take hold of its branches."
> Let now your breasts be like clusters of the vine,
> The fragrance of your breath like apples,
> And the roof of your mouth like the best wine.
> The wine goes down smoothly for my beloved,
> Moving gently the lips of sleepers.
> —SONG OF SOLOMON 7:1–3, 6–9

Among other things, the Song of Solomon is a celebration of married spiritual, emotional and sexual love.

# 18

## Sex, Society and Statistics

O UR SOCIETY HAS totally missed the point regarding sex. Unfortunately, in films and television these days, the sexual act has become as mundane and routine as eating a sandwich. Actors on film and television hop in and out of bed with each other without even a thought of the spiritual, moral and biological consequences. We live in a society that is as immoral as the ancient city of Corinth about which the apostle Paul wrote in his letter to the Corinthians. The Greek city of Corinth was famous for its sensuality and practice of prostitution, which was associated with Aphrodite, or Venus, who was the goddess of erotic love. The Temple of Aphrodite had over one thousand prostitutes who worshiped her.

It is in that context that the apostle Paul wrote these words:

> Nevertheless, because of sexual immorality, let each man have his own wife, and let each woman have her own husband. Let the husband render to his wife the affection due her, and likewise also the wife to the husband. The wife does not have authority over her own body, but the husband does. And likewise the husband does not have authority over his own body but the wife does. Do not deprive one another except with consent for a time, that you may give yourselves to fasting and prayer; and come together again so that Satan does not tempt you because of your lack of self-control. But I say this as a concession, not as a commandment. For I wish that all men were even as myself. But each one has his own gift from God, one in this manner and another in that. But I say to the unmarried and to the widows: it is good for them if they remain even as I am; but if they cannot exercise self-control, let them marry. For it is better to marry than to burn with passion.
>
> —1 CORINTHIANS 7:2–9

Paul wrote these instructions in a day very much like our own. It is important to understand that God understands the power of sexual desire within men and women. However, God has created the sexual act as something holy that should only occur between a husband and wife. One of God's functions for the marriage relationship is to satisfy sexual desires. That is why He gave these guidelines:

1.  The husband is responsible to satisfy his wife sexually.
2.  The wife is responsible to satisfy her husband sexually.
3.  The wife is to be available sexually to her husband.
4.  The husband is to be available sexually for his wife.
5.  The husband and wife are not to deny each other sexually except for rare occasions of mutual consent.
6.  Marriage is the exclusive place for sexual relations to be experienced.

The Bible gives some very strong commandments regarding sex. The husband and wife are to be totally committed to fulfilling each other sexually. One of the reasons for doing this is as a safeguard against immorality. People who are satisfied emotionally and sexually are not going to be tempted to get involved in adulterous relationships.

A word of caution needs to be added here. Hollywood and the media promote a very unrealistic view of romance, sex and passion. In the real world, people have jobs, raise children, get sick and get tired. A woman who works outside the home, works inside the home as wife and mother or does both is often going to be physically exhausted. Although the Bible tells couples to meet each other's sexual needs, balance, patience and understanding must come into this picture—especially with men. In the real world there are going to be times when a woman is totally exhausted. The last thing she may want is to be approached sexually. Men need to understand this. However, a couple must make room for sex and romance in their marriage.

## OUR BODIES ARE THE
## TEMPLE OF THE HOLY SPIRIT

There is a famous feminist book titled *Our Bodies, Ourselves*. However, nothing could be further from the truth. The basic teaching of the Bible is that your body is the temple of the Holy Spirit. In 1 Corinthians 6:19 Paul writes, "Or do you not know that your body is the temple of the Holy Spirit who is in you, whom you have from God, and you are not your own?" In other words, the Holy Spirit lives inside of every believer, and when a believer has sexual relations, the Holy Spirit is a partner in this. God created sex between a man and a woman to be pure and holy, so there is nothing wrong with the Holy Spirit being present in sexual relations between a husband and wife.

This is why the Bible does not give a list of do's and don'ts regarding human sexuality. God assumes that when two believers are filled with the Holy Spirit and walking in the Word of God, they will want to express themselves sexually in a way that glorifies Him. The Holy Spirit is in the midst of the sexual act, and in one sense, sex between a husband and wife is an act of worship to God because it is pure and holy.

When a husband and wife have sexual intercourse, they become one both spiritually and biologically. This is why God forbids sex between unmarried people. First Corinthians 6:15–18 warns against sexual immorality: "Do you not know that your bodies are members of Christ? Shall I then take members of Christ and make them members of a harlot? Certainly not! Or do you not know that he who is joined to a harlot is one body with her? For 'the two,' He says, 'shall become one flesh.' But he who is joined to the Lord is one spirit with Him. Flee sexual immorality. Every sin that a man does is outside the body, but he who commits sexual immorality sins against his own body."

The reason God reserved sex for the married man and woman is because it creates a oneness on a very deep level and a spiritual bonding between two people. This is the danger in casual sex, because casual sex is a denial of the reality of what sex is all about. Our society says that sex is casual and that it's all right to have sex with anyone of any sex whenever you want it as long as you use a condom. But God who is the Master Engineer and Designer of sex says, "No. This is not true." God warns that there are consequences to violating His commandments regarding sex—not just AIDS and other sexually transmitted diseases, but also emotional and spiritual damage.

When two people have sex, they are joined together on the spiritual dimension. Therefore, when people engage in casual sex and then quickly separate, there is a serious wounding and fragmenting of the human personality. People either block out their sensitivity to this through a hardness of heart, drugs or alcohol, or somebody gets hurt or feels abandoned and used.

It is interesting to note that after several decades of the sexual revolution, which began in the sixties, young people now seem to be desiring a return to more traditional values. A national poll taken by the Roper organization showed that more than 50 percent of the teenagers who have had sex wish that they had waited. Approximately three million American teenagers get a sexually transmitted disease each year, and around fifty thousand teenagers will get the AIDS virus because of promiscuous sex. As a result, new youth movements like "True Love Waits" are launching a counter-sexual revolution. During a "True Love Waits" rally in Washington, D.C., more than two hundred thousand teenagers signed a pledge card promising not to have sex until they were married.[1]

Sex is a gift of God to the husband and wife. The full range of powerful emotions, the physical attraction, the physical pleasures and the state of orgasm are all created by God to be fully enjoyed by the married couple. Sex for the Christian husband and wife is to be a celebration of their marriage and a means of both rich enjoyment and procreation. Even though sex is intended as a celebration, at some point in any marriage, the sexual excitement can wane. Instead of running to another person for fulfillment, the believer needs to turn again to his spouse and rekindle the flame. That's what the next chapter is all about.

# 19

## Fireworks,
## Anyone?

I**T CAN HAPPEN** in any marriage relationship—you forget why you fell in love with the other person. That's why it's so important to remember the things that made you fall in love to begin with. A marriage is like a garden. It has to be tended and cultivated; otherwise the weeds will come in and destroy the flowers. If we are not careful, the daily routines of life and the responsibilities of raising a family, money, jobs and other pressures can make even the best of marriages an ugly treadmill experience.

One of the reasons that men and women get involved in adulterous relationships (or have affairs, as society calls them) is because an individual is looking for a way to escape the pressures of life. People were not created by God to exist in a prisonlike existence without joy, creativity and fun. It is God's plan that joy, creativity and fun have room to grow within a faithful married relationship. However, when the marriage becomes neglected either through ignorance or lack of interest, the weeds of discontent and anger begin to grow.

Then when another man or woman outside the circle of the marriage enters into the picture and offers the illusion of fun, joy and creativity, Satan is given an opportunity to tempt a husband and wife into sin. However, if the garden of the marriage is tended, then neither partner will have occasion to look elsewhere for fulfillment. Unfortunately, our society, which is antimarriage in many respects, often encourages the idea of the affair as a desirable option.

The best protection against having an affair or committing adultery is to cultivate the garden of your marriage. Although somewhat crass, there is a degree of truth in the old adage: "If you have steak at home, why would you look for hamburger somewhere else?" Not that a husband or wife should ever be compared to a piece of meat, but the point is that if the marriage is fulfilling, neither husband nor wife will seek fulfillment somewhere else.

It is God's plan that men and women find total fulfillment within a holy and pure marriage relationship. It is possible to cultivate the garden of your marriage and enjoy a lifetime of intimacy, wonder, discovery and romance. The original fireworks that brought you together in the first place can be set off—and not just on the Fourth of July. It is possible to trigger those deep, romantic feelings by taking a few small steps to recreate the emotional intimacy that brought you together in the first place.

## THE ROMANTIC TRIGGER

When people are dating or courting before marriage, they instinctively do things that produce and create intimacy. Both the man and the woman are on their best behavior. They are emotionally up and totally excited to be with one another. They are afraid of doing anything that would upset the other one even in the slightest. It is absolutely amazing that during this dating period leading up to marriage people just don't seem to get tired. If they are sick you'd never know it, and they can function perfectly with little or no sleep. Their energy level is so high because the couple is literally on a romantic high produced by a change in body chemistry, which the state of being in love creates. The key in rediscovering passion, love and romance in the marriage relationship is to repeat those things that created the space for romance to happen.

## HOW A MARRIED COUPLE
## CAN REDISCOVER ROMANCE

1.  Take long walks in nature, at the beach, down a romantic street or at a park.
2.  Stop talking about bills, finances and problems with the children. Talk about fun things. Find ways to laugh together.
3.  Do things for one another that are special,

such as a man brushing his wife's hair or massaging her feet with lotion. A woman can spend time telling her husband the reasons she thinks he is so special and by creating a romantic and sexy evening where the two are alone together.

4. Take your wife out on a date and go to the movies and a restaurant.

5. Men, write your wife a poem or love note telling her why you love her.

6. Wives, when the children are not around, wear something sexy and seduce your husband.

7. Men, find ways to be romantic—candlelit dinners, flowers, tender moments, hors d'oeuvres together, lots of atmosphere around the house or when going out to eat. You don't have to spend a lot of money, but your favorite fast-food burger place is just not going to "cut it." Choose a café or some place with lots of charm.

8. Look at the night sky. Lie on a blanket in your backyard or a park that's safe and gaze at the stars. You will be amazed how changing the daily routine to a unique and extraordinary moment will open up your emotional and intimate being.

9. Turn on music and dance in your living room.

10. Light candles and create a romantic, soft environment.

11. Have your makeup done by a cosmetic specialist.
12. Pack a picnic and take a bicycle ride together.
13. Do something out of the ordinary, something creative, something that you've never done before. Allow God to expand your mind and choices in life.

*20*

## Avoiding "The Grass Is Greener on the Other Side of the Fence" Syndrome

I HAVE BEEN MARRIED to my wife Kristina for twenty-three years. I have only been married once, and it has been to her. During our marriage I have never been unfaithful to my wife. However, as a Christian man I have discovered that there are things that I must actively do to protect my marriage from the "snare [or traps] of the devil" (2 Tim. 2:26).

A Christian marriage is an earthly model of the loving relationship between Christ and the church (Eph. 5:22–32). It is the foundation of emotional, spiritual and psychological health for our entire society. The Christian marriage is the focal point of how God wants to reach out to the world and lost humanity. You see, the Christian marriage can be one of the most positive testimonies to the reality of Jesus Christ that the world can see. As such, Satan hates Christian marriages with an unholy passion, and he actively seeks to destroy them. Most marriage books do not discuss the spiritual warfare that is involved in Christian marriages. But Ephesians 6:11–12 states:

> Put on the whole armor of God, that you may be able to stand against the wiles of the devil. For we do not wrestle against flesh and blood, but against principalities, against powers, against the rulers of the darkness of this age, against spiritual hosts of wickedness in the heavenly places.

The term "wiles of the devil" means the tricks and strategies that Satan wages against believers and their marriages. In our marriages we need to take seriously the words of the apostle Paul when he wrote, "Therefore take up the whole armor of God, that you may be able to withstand in the evil day, and having done all, to stand" (Eph. 6:13).

## A PERSONAL STORY

As I said earlier, I have never been unfaithful to my wife. However, like most men I have had to be on my guard in my mind against lust and a host of other temptations in order to preserve my moral purity. I remember one particular incident a number of years ago where I could have fallen prey to the snare or trap of Satan. Things were going a little slow in my career and ministry. As such, I was somewhat depressed and emotionally low. I had allowed my spiritual armor to be somewhat put aside. As such, the enemy knew when and how to strike, and he did.

The source of my temptation began when a female coworker on my job began to pay a little more attention to me than what would have been expected during the normal course of the work routine. At first I didn't even notice it. But, very subtly, I found myself enjoying the extra attention.

It was all very "innocent" and what I believed to be harmless. But because my spiritual armor was down and I was not actively guarding my marriage, the enemy was very quietly digging his hooks in me.

Although this work relationship never progressed beyond a few conversations as I passed by this woman in the hallway, I found myself gradually becoming romantically attracted to her. As the attraction and temptation increased I suddenly realized that I had entered into an area in my emotions that was sin and not pleasing to God. Privately, I began to confess these feelings as sin and asked God to deliver me from them.

Because I had let my guard down just a little bit in what I thought was an innocent relationship, an emotional bond had developed in my mind that was still present, even though I wanted it to go away. Fortunately, I was a submitted member of a local church, The Church On The Way in Van Nuys, California. Pastor Jack Hayford encouraged men to be part of what were then called Men's Growth Seminars. At these men's meetings, Christian men were challenged to be open and accountable to other men and to pray for one another.

Many times testimonies and messages were given regarding the type of issue I was facing. I think that if I had experienced these feelings and had not heard that other strong Christian men had faced similar things, I may have given in to despair and sinned because I would have thought that it was only me who would go through something like this. Pastor Jack Hayford shared the story of how many years ago he had battled a romantic attraction to a woman working in his office and how God had delivered him of such feelings. That message was burned into my soul like fire, and it was a great source of encouragement and hope.

I knew I should have been open and accountable to the other men in the group about my situation. In addition, I should have trusted my wife enough to have opened myself up to her. However, I did not have the courage to share my problem with my wife or the men in the men's meeting. I believe this was because I allowed Satan to deceive me through my pride and shame. The enemy wants to isolate us and condemn us so that he can destroy us.

I managed to obey the principle of transparency and accountability by calling a trusted Christian friend who lived on the East Coast. I shared with him in detail about my attraction to this woman at work. God honored my willingness to confess my sin to a brother in Christ, and healing began to happen. Before we got off the phone he said he would send some written prayers in the mail that would help me to pray.

About a week later, the letter arrived from my friend on the East Coast in which he discussed my problem and shared some prayers. Since my friend was also a good friend of my wife's, when she got the letter out of the mail box, she opened it up and read it. After reading the letter she called me at work to ask me what was going on in my life. I basically covered everything up and said nothing. Then she said that she had read the letter and knew the problem I was facing.

To this day I believe that God had caused her to read that letter so that everything would be brought out in the open and I could be set free from the bondage I was in. Kristina strongly suggested that we set up an appointment for counseling with one of the associate pastors at The Church On The Way. I dreaded going to the meeting because I was filled with so much shame and guilt. I was somewhat well-known at the church because I had written a number of books and spoken there. I felt that I would "disappoint" the pastor and that he would look down on me.

Shame, guilt, pride and confusion had gripped me and actually made the situation worse. When Kristina and I met with the associate pastor, I did not experience even a hint of condemnation. In fact, he shared a personal story about some problems that he faced in his life that really helped me to become transparent. I realized that God was not angry at me and that my wife was not angry at me. I felt truly forgiven by God, and as we prayed, a great emotional weight was lifted off me.

When I met with Kristina and this pastor, I opened myself up and shared the situation I was in. At that moment a great deliverance was working in my life, and the cords of romantic attraction were finally severed. It was like waking up from a bad dream. As long as I hid my sin and failure, the enemy was free to keep me in bondage and sin. The letter falling into Kristina's hands had forced me to open up and get help from brothers and sisters in Christ. When my problem was exposed to the light of Jesus Christ in accountable and transparent relationships, its potency to destroy me was dismantled.

## THE LESSONS I LEARNED

I learned a number of important things about myself and marriage by going through this experience. First of all, I learned that I always need to have my spiritual armor on in relationship to my marriage and my spiritual life. I discovered that the words of the apostle Peter are certainly applicable to marriage when he said, "Be sober, be vigilant; because your adversary the devil walks about like a roaring lion, seeking whom he may devour" (1 Peter 5:8). There is a spiritual enemy who hates the Christian marriage, and we must stand our guard spiritually against his attacks.

Also, I discovered that when I am emotionally low or tired, I am more vulnerable to the enemy's attacks. As someone who came from a dysfunctional family where alcoholism was evident, I have discovered that I have in my own personality some addictive disorders.

God has healed me of them and transformed me, but I have certain areas of vulnerability that I need to be careful about. Before accepting Jesus Christ into my life, I used to do a lot of "partying" with drinking and drugs. I used to smoke two packs of cigarettes a day, and I definitely had an addictive personality. I believe this addictive personality was part of a generational curse passed on from my parents. Scientific evidence even backs up the idea that parents pass on psychological character traits to their children. Scientists have discovered that there are genetic predispositions to things like alcoholism passed on in our DNA from one generation to the next.

When I was emotionally low and not feeling all that great about myself, I was vulnerable. Proverbs 6:25 warns against adultery when it says, "Do not lust after her beauty in your heart, nor let her allure you with her eyelids." Subconsciously, I found it more pleasant to think about this girl because it took my mind off my problems. At the very core of this was my own personal propensity toward addictive behavior.

Since I no longer drink alcohol or take drugs to alleviate emotional pain and anxiety, developing a romantic infatuation in my mind acted like a drug and took my mind off my problems. Temporarily, it gave me a lift and a rush of excitement. Alcohol, drugs, food and sexual addictions all work in the same way. However, all these things will create spiritual bondage in a person's life.

I have learned to recognize this potential weakness in myself, and I have learned to guard against it. In addition,

I have also learned to guard my heart more carefully and not allow myself to "toy" with attraction to members of the opposite sex.

Finally, I have learned the importance of being in accountable relationships with members of the body of Christ. The enemy will seek to attack us when we are "cut off" and isolated from our brothers and sisters in Christ. My strength in marriage and in my spiritual life comes from being in fellowship with believers in a local church.

# 21

How to Affair-Proof
Your Marriage

W<small>E HAVE ALL</small> felt the sorrow, dismay and shock
when Christian leaders are forced to leave
their ministries after an affair is revealed. We squirm in
embarrassment when the media report that nationally
known contemporary gospel musicians are caught in an
"extramarital relationship." Tragically, these announce-
ments are not all that unusual these days. It is not just
secular society that is engaging in adulterous relationships. These same sins are now plaguing the church in
increasing numbers.

It is not with any tone of superspirituality that I write
about the dangerous appeal of affairs. As you read in the
last chapter, I too found myself in temptation and had to

take difficult steps to expose the problem and break the stronghold in my mind.

However, in this chapter I want to focus on specific ways husbands and wives can guard themselves against the temptation of committing sin and breaking their marriage vows.

## THE DYNAMICS OF AN AFFAIR

King Solomon, one of the wisest men who ever lived, gives us some insight into the nature of seduction, sexual immorality and adultery in Proverbs 5:1–23; 6:32–35; and 7:1–27. The perspective is primarily from a male point of view; however, many of these dynamics could fit the female perspective also, as we shall see. First, Proverbs 5:3 says, "For the lips of an immoral woman drip honey, and her mouth is smoother than oil." In this passage, we learn that the initial temptation for the man in committing adultery is the physical characteristics of the woman.

However, Solomon warns that there is a high price to pay for uncontrolled sexual desire.

> My son, pay attention to my wisdom; lend your ear to my understanding...in the end she is bitter as wormwood, sharp as a two-edged sword. Her feet go down to death, her steps lay hold of hell. Lest you ponder her path of life—her ways are unstable; you do not know them....Remove your way far from her, and do not go near the door of her house, lest you give your honor to others, and your years to the cruel one; lest aliens be filled with your wealth,

and your labor go to the house of the foreigner; and you mourn at last when your flesh and body are consumed.

—PROVERBS 5:1,4–6, 8–11

The devastating results of an adulterous relationship are spelled out as follows:

1. Loss of reputation (v. 9)
2. Other people will get your wealth (in divorce court!) (v. 10)
3. Deep sadness, remorse and regret (v. 11)
4. Diseases such as AIDS and other sexually transmitted diseases (v. 11)

God understands that every man has a will in the area of sexual temptation, and through relying on the power of God's Holy Spirit he can successfully resist these desires.

## THE MAN'S VULNERABILITY

In Proverbs 6:24–25 we learn something profound about the nature of man's vulnerability to temptation. Solomon writes, "...to keep you from the evil woman, from the flattering tongue of a seductress. Do not lust after her beauty in your heart, nor let her allure you with her eyelids." In this passage, we learn that a man is vulnerable to her flattering tongue, her physical attraction and her admiring stares. The primary area of vulnerability for the man is in the area of his ego needs. Although the sexual appeal of the woman is of key importance, the real area for temptation for the man is that the seducing woman appeals to his sense of self-worth and masculinity.

It is vital to understand this dynamic here if we are to safeguard our relationships from adultery. This immoral woman who is outside the marriage is attempting to seduce the man through meeting his needs to feel important, respected, strong and masculine. Ephesians 5:33 says, "Let the wife see that she respects her husband." In other words, the wife is supposed to make her husband feel important, respected, strong and masculine. This is a very crucial area and one that reveals the inner psychological workings of the male.

God created the woman to be a helper or helpmate to the male, according to Genesis 2:20. One of the key ways to fulfill this role is to do and say things that empower the man to feel important and respected, build up his self-worth and reinforce his masculinity. Also, the woman should not take her husband for granted and should make herself attractive to the man by taking proper care of her appearance.

If the wife neglects her husband and takes him for granted or criticizes and belittles him, then she is tearing down a hedge of protection in her marriage and opening a door where the enemy can come in. In this situation there will be an unmet need in the man that will make him particularly vulnerable to temptation when a woman outside the marriage comes in and begins to meet these needs.

However, there are many other reasons why marital infidelity can occur, and this is not in any way to suggest that the blame can be put solely on the wife. The wife may be meeting all of these needs more than adequately, and yet the husband still falls into temptation. Because of the Fall and man's sin nature, the husband may choose not to yield to the Spirit of Christ but walk in the flesh and therefore open himself up to temptation because of lust, carnality and covetousness.

The most important safeguard against a man having an affair is a strong walk with Jesus Christ. However, the wife does have a duty and responsibility to build him up. Below are some specific things she can do:

## SPECIFIC ACTIONS OF LOVE THE WIFE CAN DO FOR HER HUSBAND

1. Build him up as a man with her words
2. Respect him
3. Believe in him
4. Think the best of him
5. Pray for him
6. Encourage him
7. Praise him for his good qualities
8. Admire him
9. Make herself sexually attractive to him
10. Take time to make herself sexually available to him

11. Take an interest and joy in her sexual relationship with him (don't do it out of duty or obligation)
12. Delight in him as a man

### THE WOMAN'S VULNERABILITY

While the man seems particularly vulnerable in the area of his ego needs, the woman is also very vulnerable on a number of levels. Although physical attraction is important, a woman also needs a man to be sensitive, caring, romantic, tender, gentle, fun and emotionally intimate. If a husband is not meeting his wife's needs in these areas, then the woman can be tempted to find emotional satisfaction outside the marriage.

In our day, when the number of married women going to work has risen 65 percent since 1970, a whole new sociological framework has been developed. Women, like men, regularly meet members of the opposite sex in the workplace. In addition, the soap opera mentality of casual relationships is hammered home day after day via the mass media.

The man is "turned on" primarily by physical appearance and when a woman builds him up and is an interesting companion as well. A woman is motivated by romance, intimate communication, acts of kindness, tenderness and a man who shows genuine interest in her as a person and not just a "sex object."

Ephesians 5:25 tells men to love their wives, and this theme is repeated numerous times in Ephesians 5:22–33.

In practical terms, a man loves his wife by doing the following actions.

## SPECIFIC ACTIONS OF LOVE
## THE HUSBAND CAN DO

1. Listen to his wife
2. Be physically tender by caressing her, brushing her hair, massaging her, holding her hand and so forth
3. Buy her flowers
4. Write her love notes and poems
5. Compliment her appearance and tell her how beautiful she is
6. Go on romantic walks
7. Let her in your life and talk to her
8. Share your innermost feelings with her
9. Pray for her needs daily and tell her
10. Be interested in her feelings
11. Find out how to meet her sexual needs
12. Be specific in telling her why she is important to you
13. Do an activity that is totally unique; allow God to inspire you.

When the husband demonstrates his love for his wife in practical ways, he is meeting her deepest needs and is blessing her as his wife. In addition, he is allowing no place for the devil in terms of temptation because he is building a hedge of emotional protection around her.

First Corinthians 7:5 says, "Do not deprive one another except with consent for a time, that you may give yourselves to fasting and prayer; and come together again so that Satan does not tempt you because of your lack of self control." Although this passage of scripture is talking about the need for the husband and wife to have sexual relations regularly, the principle could be applied to the emotional and psychological needs of the man and woman as well.

Just as when the devil is given opportunity to tempt the husband and wife when they do not meet each other's physical needs, so also Satan can come in if the husband and wife are neglecting each other in the emotional and psychological areas. Adultery doesn't just happen, and affairs don't just materialize out of thin air. Oftentimes there has been neglect by one or both of the partners. This neglect leads to an opportunity for Satan to arrange a situation to tempt either the husband and wife. Satan hates the testimony of Christian marriages, and he delights in causing someone to sin.

The Christian husband and wife need to understand that they are not just two people who are married. If they are walking with the Lord and are filled with His Holy Spirit, then their marriage is a living testimony to the reality and goodness of Jesus Christ. As such, their marriage and family are going to experience spiritual warfare. This is not to blame everything on the devil. But it is to give an honest recognition of the fact that the enemy would love to see this testimony of Christ destroyed and to bring down their marriage.

We must remember that our whole world is under the sway of the evil one, and that the mass media with its books, television, movies, magazines, music and culture literally scream at believers to participate in its immorality. Unless we are filled with the Spirit, reading the Word daily and submitted to a church, we are going to be very vulnerable to the enemy's strategies. Let's take our ministries to our spouses very seriously and meet their needs on every level. This is love in action, and it prevents the enemy from getting a foothold in our marriages and families.

# Section V
# Man to Man

## 22

---

# The Role of the
# Man in Marriage

**T**HE BIBLICAL CONCEPT that the man is supposed to be the head of the home and that the wife is supposed to submit to the husband is one of the most misunderstood and often abused truths in the Bible. It is true that the Bible calls men to be the "head of the wife," but the man is the head of the wife the same way that "Christ is the head of the church" (Eph. 5:23). The key concept is that Jesus Christ literally sacrificed His very life for the church that He loves.

The Bible teaches that the man is to be head of the wife and home as a servant who does not "lord it over" his wife and children, but who constantly lays down his life and own selfish interests in order to serve them with a heart filled with love. This concept of headship through servanthood is a revolutionary and radical concept that is only found in the Bible.

What women have been reacting to for centuries and more recently within the modern feminist movement is the false idea of male supremacy. Nowhere does the Bible teach that man is superior over the woman. Ephesians 5:21–32 places such an enormous responsibility on the man to love, serve and cherish his wife that no one properly interpreting the scripture could say that the Bible teaches male superiority or male chauvinism.

Starting in Genesis 3:16 we learn something about God's redemptive plan for both men and women:

> To the woman He said: "I will greatly multiply your sorrow and your conception; in pain you shall bring forth children; your desire shall be for your husband, and he shall rule over you."

Genesis 3:16 gives the husband the assignment to be the servant-head of the marriage relationship. This passage of Scripture does not say that men are to dominate women or that men are superior to women. It simply suggests that in the marriage relationship the man is to be the servant-leader. In no way was God suggesting that the woman not be able to fully utilize her talents or abilities.

In Ephesians 5:22–33 we learn what God intended for both men and women when He said the man was to be the "head of the wife." It is important that we understand exactly what this role as head actually means and what it does not mean.

## WHAT THE BIBLE MEANS WHEN IT ASSIGNS MEN AS LEADERS IN THE MARRIAGE AND THE HOME

1.  Men are to be servant-leaders.
2.  Men are to place the needs and desires of their wives and children above their own.
3.  As leaders, men are to sacrifice their lives for their wives and children.
4.  Men are not to exercise leadership for selfish purposes but rather in a spirit of giving.
5.  The power of a man's leadership comes from the degree that he is willing to serve and not be served.
6.  The ultimate act of biblical leadership or headship is laying down your life, needs and wants for those of your family.
7.  Men and women are equal but have different roles.

## WHAT THE BIBLE DOES NOT MEAN WHEN IT ASSIGNS MEN AS LEADERS IN MARRIAGE AND THE HOME

1.  The head or leadership is not to be confused with being the "boss." The man is to be the servant-leader, not the "boss" in the traditional sense of the word.
2.  The man is not to expect his wife and children to serve him or meet his needs, desires and wants. He is to serve and not be served.
3.  The man is not to seek to control, manipulate

or assert his own authority over his wife and children. His authority comes from his own yieldedness to Jesus Christ.

4. The man is not to think of himself as "king of the castle," but rather the servant-leader of the castle.

5. A man's motivation in being head of the home should always be one of self-giving love and not that of a taker.

6. A man should not expect his wife and children to "bow down to him."

7. Men are not superior to females.

8. Men are not over females.

## WE HAVE THE WHOLE THING BACKWARDS

The Bible's teaching on the man being the head of the home has been completely misunderstood more often than not. Without question the Bible teaches that the man is the head and leader of the home. However, it is a leadership based on total accountability to Jesus Christ and a leadership that is based entirely on servanthood. Statements like the following completely miss the point:

- "Show her who's boss."
- "Grab the bull by the horns."
- "Who wears the pants?"
- "Meet the boss" (when a man points to his wife).

In John 12:24–26 we get a good description of the kind of servanthood Jesus Christ was calling for. It is a totally radical and revolutionary approach that, when practiced, creates amazing results—but it costs everything.

> Most assuredly, I say to you, unless a grain of wheat falls into the ground and dies, it remains alone; but if it dies, it produces much grain. He who loves his life will lose it, and he who hates his life in this world will keep it for eternal life. If anyone serves Me, let him follow Me; and where I am, there My servant will be also. If anyone serves Me, him My Father will honor.

Jesus demonstrates the need for self-sacrifice, love and servanthood (Luke 22:24–27; John 3:34–35; 13:3–17). When God calls a man to be head of his home, it is precisely these kind of servant-leader traits that are called for.

# 23

# Responsibilities
# of the Husband

I N ISAIAH 54:5 the prophet writes, "For your Maker is your husband, the LORD of Hosts is His name; and your Redeemer is the Holy One of Israel; He is called the God of the whole earth." In this passage, God is described to His people as a husband who both protects and provides. The entire Bible communicates that the God of the universe is not just some abstract mystical force, but a personal and living God. In addition, God is a father and a husband to His people.

Out of this reality that God is both father and husband come the model and identity for Christian husbands and fathers. It is only because we have a heavenly Father that it is possible for men to become the husbands and fathers

God created us to be. This is one of the reasons why the theory of evolution proposed by Charles Darwin (1809–1882) is so destructive—not just because it is scientifically untrue, but because it is impossible for any man to be a true father and husband out of the chaos and chance that evolution promotes. Being a husband and father flows directly out of the reality of God's existence. The Bible very clearly teaches the duties and responsibilities of the husband.

### Responsibility 1: A husband must provide for his family.

Although the number of moms leaving home for work each morning continues to rise, God designed the family for the man to be the leader in terms of providing for the family. However, in today's world where the average family pays about 40 percent of their income to taxes as compared to about 4.5 percent in 1950, it is increasingly necessary for both husband and wife to work.

The structure of our tax system is antifamily; it was never God's intention for families to be so burdened financially that both parents would have to work. In addition, along with the increased number of mothers working, there is an increase of children being raised by day care.

Even if the wife earns more than the husband, according to the Bible, the husband should still provide the financial leadership of the family as "head of the home."

159

## *Responsibility 2: The husband is to set the emotional tone for the home.*

The husband's moods, attitude and state of mind have a profound impact on the marriage and the family. As the leader, he must make sure that he leads in terms of the emotional atmosphere of the home and family. This means he cannot give in to being moody, depressed, angry, sullen and quick. He will have those feelings when he is emotionally low, angry or even upset. However, the key is that the husband is not to indulge himself in these moods.

The only way that the husband can set the emotional tone for the marriage and home is to be filled with the Holy Spirit (Eph. 5:18). Intense moodiness is a work of the flesh. The only way for a husband to have love, joy, peace, longsuffering, kindness, goodness, faithfulness, gentleness and self-control—the fruit of the Spirit listed in Galatians 5:22–23—is to walk in the power of the Holy Spirit.

## *Responsibility 3: The husband is to be the spiritual leader.*

Many men let their wives be the spiritual leader of the home. Yet the man is supposed to be the spiritual head of the home. This means he is to lead in having regular family devotions, Bible study, prayer, fasting and going to church. Ephesians 5:26 says, "...that He might sanctify and cleanse her with the washing of water by the word." Paul was comparing the relationship of Jesus Christ with the church to the relationship between a husband and wife. So when Paul talks about Jesus cleansing and sanctifying the church with the Word of God, he is also indicating that the husband should cleanse and sanctify his home with the Word of God. The husband should read the Word of God in his home and allow its cleansing power to permeate his household and marriage relationship.

### Responsibility 4: The husband is to be the romancer of the wife.

Just as in courtship when the man pursued his wife romantically, the husband is to take leadership in continuing to pursue her romantically after they are married. It is the man's responsibility to continue to "court" his wife after they are married. This means he is to do the same kinds of things he did for her before they were married, such as buying her flowers, love notes, cards, dressing up, taking her out, praising her, holding her hand, caressing her hair, telling her how beautiful she is, walking with her and holding her hand.

If a man neglects his wife romantically and begins to take her for granted, then he is accountable to God for this marital neglect. The romance should continue between the husband and wife for all the days they are married here on earth.

### Responsibility 5: The husband must love and nurture his wife.

In addition to courting his wife, the husband must take active steps in loving his wife. This means being sensitive to her special needs, listening to her, looking out for her and meeting her emotional needs. The husband must understand that his wife is different than he is. He must take the time to really find out what her needs are and listen to her.

The rule is that the husband must actually "love his own wife as himself" (Eph. 5:33). That means he must think about her needs, desires, wants, likes and dislikes more than he does his own. He must devote time and attention not only to thinking about what his wife needs and wants, but also devote time and energy to meeting her needs. In the sexual area, this means not just thinking about his own wants and desires, but how he can please her.

### Responsibility 6: The husband must be the priest of the home.

The husband is responsible not only to be the spiritual leader of the home, but also to be the priest of the home. This means that he must daily pray for his wife and children. Although the husband and wife may pray together, it is the husband who must daily present his wife and children before the throne room of God, intercede for them, pray for their supernatural protection and speak blessing on them.

It is primarily the husband who must surround his home and marriage with a hedge of supernatural protection through intercessory prayer (Mark 12:1). He must bind the power of the adversary (Matt. 16:19). Many tragedies could be avoided in the home and marriage if only the husband took his rightful place as intercessor.

162

In Genesis 27:27–29 we read the account of Isaac blessing his son. In other passages of the Bible we read accounts of men of God blessing their children. Blessing is a release of supernatural favor and protection on people.

God has given the husband the supernatural authority to bless his wife and children through speaking blessing and by laying hands upon them. Although the wife can also release blessing in her family, the husband has been given the central role in imparting blessing supernaturally. When a man releases blessing on his wife and family, there is an anointing of the Holy Spirit that attends that divine act. It is an actual impartation of divine energy and force that carries healing, favor, abundance and grace.

To sum it all up, John W. Whitehead, who is a constitutional attorney and president of the Rutherford Institute, writes:

> Men need to shed arrogant, macho posturing and help their wives, even if that means staying at home and performing tasks thought of as "wifely" functions. Jesus Christ set the example by washing the feet of His disciples. In view of Jesus Christ's great sacrifice, surely the Christian husband can love his wife sacrificially. To do less is simply wrong. The wife is a full partner, equal to her husband in every way.[1]

## HOW THE HUSBAND'S ACTIONS PRODUCE SPECIFIC RESPONSES IN THE WIFE

### HUSBAND'S ACTION:

| | |
|---|---|
| LACK OF LEADERSHIP | Either through neglect, ignorance or fear, the husband fails to provide real leadership spiritually, emotionally or financially to shelter and protect the wife. |
| Violation of Ephesians 5:23 | "For the husband is head of the wife, as also Christ is head of the church; and He is the Savior of the Body." God commands the husband to exercise leadership, or headship, in the home. |

### WIFE'S RESPONSE:

| | |
|---|---|
| COMPLAINING | The wife begins to nag, nitpick, complain and say things designed to get the husband to assume his biblical role as head of the house. |

### HUSBAND'S ACTION:

| | |
|---|---|
| INSENSITIVE | The husband is not tuned in to the wife's needs, wants and desires. He is in his own world and is not really paying attention to his wife's verbal communication and her signals. |
| Violation of Ephesians 5:25 | "Husbands, love your wives, just as Christ also loved the church and gave Himself for her." The husband must serve his wife; his number one ministry in life is to minister to her and his family. A husband is responsible before God to meet his wife's needs. Before he can meet those needs, he must discover what they are through listening and really paying attention. He cannot afford to be oblivious to what is going on in her life. |

### WIFE'S RESPONSE:

| | |
|---|---|
| MOODY | The wife reacts by either becoming angry, depressed, emotionally withdrawn and sexually unresponsive to the husband. |

## HUSBAND'S ACTION:

UNTRUSTWORTHY The basic problem here is that the husband's word does not mean anything. He says he will do something but does not follow through. He cannot be trusted or counted on.

Violation
Ephesians 5:28

"So husbands ought to love their own wives as their own bodies; he who loves his wife loves himself." The husband must make his wife's needs a priority above his own. When a man promises his wife something, it must take on the same importance as something that is "near and dear" to him. All of us do what is really important to us. The issue is the husband making his wife's needs as important as his own. This requires a complete change of heart that only Christ can give.

## WIFE'S RESPONSE:

NAGGING The wife constantly brings up things the husband has failed to do and keeps a score of the husband's record of past failures.

## HUSBAND'S ACTION:

LACK OF
SENSITIVITY

The husband is not tuned in to his wife's emotional state, needs and wants. This does not come naturally for the majority of men. It is something the man must train himself to do.

Violation
1 Peter 3:7

"Husbands, likewise, dwell with them with understanding, giving honor to the wife, as to the weaker vessel." The woman is not inferior or second-class to the man. However, she is different, and as such she needs the strength of the man in order to be whole. Just as a flower is dependent on the sunshine and water in order to grow, so the wife must have regular spiritual, psychological and emotional nourishment from her husband.

## WIFE'S RESPONSE:

SEXUALLY
UNRESPONSIVE

When the wife is continually ignored emotionally, she will either be unresponsive sexually or merely "go through the motions" without really enjoying intimacy with her husband.

165

# 24

# The Husband's Personal Checklist

C LEARLY, THE TASK of being a husband is so awesome that the only way any man can accomplish this is through a continual reliance on the Spirit's power. Let's review three of the passages of Scripture in Ephesians that give husbands a specific responsibility in treating their wives properly.

> Husbands, love your wives, just as Christ also loved the church and gave Himself for her.
> —EPHESIANS 5:25

> So husbands ought to love their own wives as their own bodies; he who loves his wife loves himself.
> —EPHESIANS 5:28

Nevertheless let each one of you in particular so love his own wife as himself, and let the wife see that she respects her husband.

—EPHESIANS 5:33

These are all pretty heavy verses for the husband. They basically tell the man that he needs to die completely to his self-centered ways and love his wife as much as he loves himself. In expanding our awareness concerning how well we are fulfilling Christ's commission to love our wives, the following checklist may be helpful. After completing the checklist, we might want to have our wives complete it also to evaluate us, and we can compare her perception to our own.

Answer YES or NO to each question below:

1.  Do you honestly spend time each day thinking of ways to meet her needs as well as your own?
    ❑ Yes   ❑ No

2.  Do you pray for your wife daily?
    ❑ Yes   ❑ No

3.  Would your wife say that you know how to listen?
    ❑ Yes   ❑ No

4.  Would your wife say that you really understand her?
    ❑ Yes   ❑ No

5.  Would your wife say that you are her best friend?
    ❑ Yes   ❑ No

6. Are you always available to your wife when she needs you?
   ❑ Yes   ❑ No

7. When you have sexual relations with your wife, are you thinking of ways to meet her needs or your own?
   ❑ Yes   ❑ No

8. Do you praise your wife regularly?
   ❑ Yes   ❑ No

9. Would your wife say that you always say that you're sorry and admit it when you are wrong?
   ❑ Yes   ❑ No

10. Do you criticize your wife?
    ❑ Yes   ❑ No

11. Would you rather spend time alone with your wife than do any other thing?
    ❑ Yes   ❑ No

12. Can your wife correct you without you getting defensive or mad?
    ❑ Yes   ❑ No

13. Do you make your wife feel special and good about herself?
    ❑ Yes   ❑ No

14. Would your wife say that you are romantic?
    ❑ Yes   ❑ No

15. Would your wife say that you are a good leader?
    ❑ Yes   ❑ No

# 25

# Meeting the Emotional
# Needs of Your Wife

WHEN GOD CREATED men and women He knew that they were different and had individual needs. God created the husband to be the spiritual leader of the marriage and the family (Eph. 5:23). As a leader, he must look out for the needs of his wife and children. In order to do that, he must understand and be sensitive to their needs.

The day our oldest child Paul started kindergarten was a difficult situation for Kristina. Before kindergarten we had sent Paul to a small Christian preschool where the teacher was a Christian and religious subjects were taught. Now we had to send him to a brand-new public school just a few blocks from our house. It was clear that there would be no Christian instruction of any kind at this school.

When all three of our small children were going to a Christian school, Kristina would write on their brown lunch bags something like "Jesus loves you, Paul, and I love you. Mom." The very first day we sent our oldest child to public school, Kristina wrote on the younger kids' lunch bags: "Jesus loves you, Michael, and I love you. Mom." "Jesus loves you, Jennifer, and I love you. Mom." However, on Paul's lunch bag she simply wrote "I love you. Mom." Those words symbolized everything because the words "Jesus loves you" were conspicuously absent.

It's not that we are embarrassed or ashamed to write the words "Jesus loves you" on his lunch bag. Neither Kris or I are ashamed of letting people know we are Christians. However, we did not feel it was wise for Paul to enter a new school environment with such an out-front religious statement. Again, it's not a matter of attempting to hide our witness for Christ, but rather a matter of conducting ourselves with wisdom. Yet this act symbolized the entire conflict and pain we were experiencing.

Kristina said she felt as if we were offering up our child to Baal, who was the god of the heathen nations around ancient Israel. In Baal worship, these heathen nations actually engaged in child sacrifices to their idols. Here we were giving our child to a totally secular and humanistic institution where the word "Jesus" will never be heard except as a swear word. In addition, the values of the vast majority of the parents are materialistic and sensual. For many of these people their only priorities are how big their house is and whether they are driving the newest Lexus.

After kindergarten, Kristina and I sent our children to a private Christian school. It is a real financial sacrifice, but we feel that it is what God wants us to do. However, as the leader of the family I needed to be sensitive to Kristina and this whole situation. I needed to really key in to the fact that Kristina had told me: "I feel vulnerable with the children about their education and their day-to-day events."

In order to meet my wife's needs as God wanted me to, I needed to actually discipline my mind and focus in on the situation with Paul attending a secular kindergarten for the first time. It's not that I am not interested or concerned. But, like many males, I have a real tendency to be preoccupied and in my "own little world." However, in order to be the real spiritual leader I have to actively zero in on being there for my wife and children in situations like this.

As the head of the house I need to be sensitive to my wife's vulnerability and allow her to rest on my strength. In short, I need to be an emotional shelter for her. In this situation with my son Paul and his going to kindergarten, I had to do the following things in order to protect my wife and meet her needs in an area of vulnerability. Ironically, as I was writing these words on my computer, I was interrupted by a phone call where the caller said, "Hi, I'm S.A. from the *Daily News*. Are you the head of the house?" And then she tried to sell me a newspaper subscription.

Although she was just trying to sell me a newspaper subscription, her question was a good one. "Am I the head of the house?" If I am, then I must do the things that God requires in order to be the head of the house. In this situation with my son Paul, I needed to do the following:

1. I needed to actually show up and physically be there the first day he went to kindergarten.
2. I needed to listen to my wife's questions and become involved in the situation.
3. I needed to pray for my son and the whole event.
4. I needed to provide leadership by asking questions of the teacher and taking steps to ensure my son's safety and well-being.

This situation, like many other situations in a marriage and family, require that the husband become actively involved. Men often have a tendency to be passive and "dump things off on the wife." Since male passivity is encouraged by our culture, it is important for men to be on their guard against being passive and instead choose to become involved. Too often men have become encouraged to be "couch potatoes" who sit in front of the television watching a football game or get lost in their personal computer. Real manhood involves showing up and leading.

# Section VI
# Woman to Woman

*26*

# The Role of
# the Woman
# in Marriage

I T IS IMPORTANT to understand that the woman was not
created as an inferior creature. Genesis 2:18 states,
"And the LORD God said, 'It is not good that man should
be alone; I will make him a helper comparable to him.'"
One of the woman's primary roles was to be a helper to
the man. However, the word *helper* does not mean assis-
tant or servant. The word *helper* means that Adam was
not complete in and of himself. The man was created to
be in partnership with the woman. Unfortunately, there
have been some who have attempted to make the Bible
say that the woman's only reason for living is to serve
the man. This is not what the Bible is teaching. The
woman is a coequal with the man, but she has a

different set of responsibilities than the man.

## OUT OF ADAM'S RIB

In Genesis 2:21–25 we read the story of how the woman was created by God. This account is not a fairy tale or myth; it is a real space/time/history account of how the first woman was created.

> And the LORD God caused a deep sleep to fall on Adam, and he slept; and He took one of his ribs, and closed up the flesh in its place. Then the rib which the LORD God had taken from the man He made into a woman, and He brought her to the man. And Adam said: "This is bone of my bones and flesh of my flesh; she shall be called Woman, because she was taken out of Man." Therefore a man shall leave his father and mother and be joined to his wife, and they shall become one flesh. And they were both naked, the man and his wife, and were not ashamed.

We should not be surprised at how God chose to create the woman anymore than we should be surprised at the parting of the Red Sea and the resurrection of Jesus Christ. In modern scientific terms, Adam's rib would have contained all the DNA material necessary to make a woman.

God is communicating something powerful in this Genesis account that we don't want to miss. Originally, back at the beginning of time, God created the female out of the man. So they were originally one flesh. That helps us to see why God said later that when a man is united to his wife "they shall become one flesh" (Gen. 2:24).

There is a beautiful interdependent relationship between man and woman. The woman was originally inside the man. In marriage, the man goes inside the female during sexual intercourse and a baby may be conceived. If the child is male, then a male actually grows inside a female. At birth, the male comes out from the inside of a female. There is a deep biological and spiritual oneness here.

## AFTER THE FALL

After the Fall of man in the Garden of Eden, some fundamental things changed in the relationship between Adam and Eve. Genesis 1:28 says, "Then God blessed them, and God said to them, 'Be fruitful and multiply; fill the earth and subdue it; have dominion...'" In other words, both Adam and Eve were to take control over their environment and rule over it. They were co-rulers. When they sinned by disobeying God, they lost this authority and rulership.

When Adam and Eve lost their authority to rule because of sin, the nature of their relationship changed. God said to the woman, "I will greatly multiply your sorrow and your conception; in pain you shall bring forth children; your desire shall be for your husband, and he shall rule over you" (Gen. 3:16). Instead of being co-rulers, the man now ruled over the woman. Some Bible scholars believe that the phrase "your desire shall be for your husband" refers to Eve remembering her co-ruler status in the Garden of Eden and desiring to dominate her husband.

If this is true, this might be a partial explanation of the seductive power of the feminist movement to modern women because it speaks to the deep desire in the woman to regain her status as co-ruler.

After the Fall, both man and woman lost their authority. However, the biblical plan for the re-establishment of that authority is never based on self-assertion. For both the man and woman, the key to regaining authority and rulership is through submission to the will and plan of God. The man is not superior to the woman and the woman is not inferior to the man, yet they have different roles. Genesis 3:16 says, "And he shall rule over you." The man has been assigned the role of being the head of the wife. Ephesians 5:22–23 states, "Wives, submit to your own husbands, as to the Lord. For the husband is head of the wife, as also Christ is head of the church; and He is the Savior of the Body."

The truth here is that the woman is responsible to submit to the husband as the head of the relationship, but the man, who must be in submission to Jesus Christ, is to serve and lay down his life for the wife. There is no room here for the domination or exploitation of women. In addition, both the man and the woman are called to surrender their wills to the will of God. It is only in this way of surrender and submission to the will of God that both the man's and the woman's true authority can be re-established.

God's eventual purpose is to bring about Revelation 5:10, where it says, "And [you] have made us kings and priests to our God; and we shall reign on the earth." God is re-establishing the dominion and partnership that

Adam and Eve had in the Garden. The husband and wife are co-rulers in life as they are properly submitted to God and each other and the wife is in submission to the husband as the head of the home.

Sarah, the wife of Abraham, is a model of submission. Originally, Sarah's name was Sarai, which means "Princess." But God changed her name to Sarah, which means "Queen" (Gen. 17:15). With this name change, God was saying that Sarah had become a co-ruler with her husband, Abraham. Remember, God changed Abram's name to Abraham, signifying that he would become the father of many nations.

As Sarah chose to be in submission to her husband, and as God entered into a covenant relationship with Abraham and Sarah, God changed their identities and their self-image completely. As Sarah entered a right relationship with God and her husband, she was released to enter a position of co-rulership with Abraham, which her name change to Sarah signifies. Therefore, when a woman submits like Sarah, she enters the divine chain of command and becomes a co-ruler in life with her husband, or a "Queen," if you like.

John Whitehead, founder and head of the Rutherford Institute, gives us needed insight into this biblical order when he writes:

> Other biblical injunctions deal with a current problem
> in the church. Many Christian men imprison their
> wives in the house and treat them like slaves. Such

behavior runs counter to the high estate placed upon women in the Bible and in particular, to the reverent relationship men are to have with women. The Proverbs 31 "virtuous wife" is a good example of how God views women. This chapter of the Bible clearly indicates that women (including wives) are to be afforded a great deal of respect. For example, in Proverbs 31:16, the wife owns property and acts as a business person. This biblical view runs counter to the way women are often treated in Christian circles today.[1]

## THE DYNAMICS OF SUBMISSION

The basic command of God to the woman is that she is to be in submission to the husband. This is a difficult concept for many modern women, and its difficulty is amplified because even within many quarters of the Christian church the nature of submission is not properly understood.

The *Spirit-Filled Life Bible* defines *submitting* as "taking the divinely ordered place in a relationship. Submission can never be required by one human being of another; it can only be given on the basis of trust, that is, to believe God's Word and be willing to learn and grow in relationships."[2]

Dr. Jack W. Hayford says that, "The spirit of submission, whereby a woman voluntarily acknowledges her husband's leadership responsibility, is an act of faith. The Bible nowhere 'submits' or subordinates women to men generically. But this text calls a woman to submit herself to her husband (Eph. 5:22), and the husband is charged to lovingly give himself to caring for his wife—never exploiting the trust of her submission."[3]

Although God calls the woman to submit to her husband in faith, there are many checks and balances. If a man abuses or misuses his authority, then God will literally not answer or hear his prayers. "Husbands, likewise, dwell with them in understanding, giving honor to the wife, as to the weaker vessel, and as being heirs together of the grace of life, that your prayers may not be hindered" (1 Pet. 3:7).

In addition, a woman is never called to submit to a husband who is being physically, emotionally or sexually abusive.

In our day of women's liberation, the woman's call to submit to her husband is easily misunderstood. However, it is really a call to live under divine authority just as the husband must do. In fact, the Christian, whether man or woman, is a person who is living a life under the lordship of Jesus Christ. They are people who are accountable to the personal, living God of the universe. This whole contemporary idea that we own our own bodies and lives is ridiculous. Whether you choose to believe in Jesus Christ or not, you are living on borrowed time. You inhabit briefly a body that you did not create and that will give out in time. To think you own your own body or a baby in your womb is philosophically absurd.

Edith Schaeffer, the author of *A Celebration of Marriage* and wife of the late Dr. Francis Schaeffer, writes:

There is so very much talk about people owning their own bodies today—especially by women who claim that they have the right to do not only what they want sexually, but to make their bodies a graveyard for their own children, the relative that is closest to them. For a Christian, all the talk about a "right to my body" is all wrong! Our bodies belong to the One who died so that we can have transformed bodies that will be perfect in eternity. They have been paid for by Jesus, and we need to study how we are supposed to use them, and recognize sin and ask forgiveness for what we have done wrong with our bodies.[4]

It is only when we really understand the way the universe works that we can find freedom. True freedom and fulfillment can only come about when we live in divine order by submitting to the plan and purposes of God.

When a woman submits to her husband, she is really submitting to the Lord. By taking her place in the divine order, she makes room for God to deal with her husband's heart. Submission is like many other biblical principles—it requires faith. When a woman submits to her husband's authority, she is stepping out in faith and obeying God. She is trusting that God will protect her and cover her through her husband.

## WHAT THE BIBLE MEANS WHEN IT CALLS WOMEN TO SUBMIT TO THEIR HUSBANDS

1. The wife submits to her husband's leadership

and gives him the final say in decision making. The Bible is not calling for "blind obedience." The woman can have an active role in the decision-making process because the husband and wife are partners. However, the final direction for the home and family is up to the husband. It should be noted that the wise husband closely pays attention to his wife's counsel.

2. The wife is to respect her husband's leadership and honor him as head of the home (Eph. 5:23).

3. The wife must trust that when she is in submission to her husband, God will deal with his heart and bring about any necessary changes. The wife's duty of submission is not based on her husband making the "right" decision every time, but on God's divine order. As the husband and wife learn to partner together in life, this decision-making process becomes a joint venture and a cooperative one.

## WHAT THE BIBLE DOES NOT MEAN WHEN IT CALLS WIVES TO SUBMIT TO THEIR HUSBANDS

1. The wife is not called to be the "doormat" of the husband. She is equal to the husband, but has a different role.

2. The wife is not to be abused either emotionally, physically or sexually.

3. Submission is not to be confused with being the lesser party. The wife is still to play an

active role in the decision-making process.

4. The wife is not a second-class citizen in any way.

5. The biblical view of the woman is someone who can be a person of authority and power. Proverbs 31:16 shows us an example of a woman who owns property and has a business. Although the woman is to be in submission to the husband within the marriage relationship, she is free to exercise spiritual and leadership gifts in the workplace and in ministry.

## 27

How to Submit
to a Jerk

WITHOUT A DOUBT, the Bible teaches that women are to submit to their husbands. But as Christian men, we often through our self-centeredness and insensitivity abuse this principle. My wife, Kristina, remembers quite well the time when at forty years of age she had just given birth to twins. In addition, she was recovering from incredible fatigue and sickness. One day, a number of family and friends had gathered downstairs to visit her. On her way down the stairs, she placed her hand on the wall because she could barely stand up. In typical mode of complete male insensitivity, I reminded her not to put her hands on the wall.

I was oblivious to her fatigue, stress and sickness, and

seemed myopically preoccupied with her dirtying the wall. So the question is, When men are "jerks"—which most of us have been known to be—how does a wife submit to a jerk? Is the Bible giving men a blank check to be selfish, inconsiderate and demanding? I don't think so, but that is how a lot of men interpret Ephesians 5:22. They completely forget Ephesians 5:25: "Husbands, love your wives, just as Christ also loved the church and gave Himself for her."

The word *submission* sends terror into the hearts of Christian women in homes all across America. Why? Because in some cases, their husbands are basically acting like jerks. So the question is, Are they still required to submit?

To answer that question, let's review God's pattern for submission in the marriage relationship. Biblical submission requires a number of things besides the wife simply submitting to her husband. Ephesians 5:21 states, "...submitting to one another in the fear of the Lord." In other words, in addition to the wife submitting to the husband, the husband and wife as believers are to submit to one another in the Lord. That means they are to defer to one another and get each other's input in making decisions and choices.

Also, the husband is to be in submission to the lordship of Jesus Christ. In all things the husband is to submit to God's directions and guidance. The husband's authority as the head of the home flows directly out of his own personal relationship and submission to Jesus Christ.

So the biblical principle of submission involves a

number of things—the husband and wife submitting to each other, the husband's submission to Jesus Christ and the wife submitting herself to the husband. This does not negate the fact that the husband is the head of the wife and the head of the home. God has established a divine order in the marriage relationship.

## PROBLEMS IN SUBMISSION

The wife submitting to her husband was never supposed to be some weird medieval principle where the wife is treated like a servant or slave. Yet I have seen many contemporary Christian marriages where the concept of submission is played out in some bizarre legalistic manner where the wife acts like some kind of timid slave to her husband.

When the Bible talks about submission, it is not talking about putting the wife in some kind of psychological bondage. Women are not second-class citizens. The principle of submission should set both the wife and husband free. It should be a joyous thing that lifts emotional burdens and pressures off the wife and allows the man to fulfill his God-given responsibility of leadership.

So the question remains, How does a woman submit to her husband if he is a jerk? Let's face it, there are some men out there (as well as women) who can be pretty nasty and ugly. God never calls a woman to be abused pyschologically or sexually. Yet there are times in a marriage relationship when a husband may be insensitive and make the wrong decisions.

As a general rule, a wife is supposed to submit to her husband. That does not mean that she does not have the right to disagree with him and tell him that she believes he is wrong about something. However, the man is the head of the house, and ultimately it is he who must make the final decision. If a man's decision is going to seriously harm his wife or children, God does not require the wife to go along blindly. It may be well advised for her to get her pastor or some other recognized Christian leader involved.

But there are some times the wife will have to submit to her husband's authority even if she thinks he is wrong. The important thing to remember is that when a wife is in genuine and heartfelt submission to her husband, God's power can be released to change her husband if he is out of order. Being in submission to divine authority releases kingdom power to change the husband and deal with his heart.

When a wife is in rebellion or refuses to submit to her husband, then God's power can actually be hindered by the woman's rebellion. In a similar manner, when we work for someone else we may have a boss or manager whom we do not like. Yet God requires that we be in submission to that individual and pray for them. We may not always agree with the decision that our boss makes, but if we want to keep our jobs, we follow orders whether we agree or disagree.

Certainly, this analogy has limitations, because we can always quit our jobs and find new ones. The point is that in the marriage relationship the wife may have to submit to her husband's decisions even if she does not always agree. In addition, her husband may be acting like a complete jerk. Yet, within the bounds of not being abused or injured, the wife is required to submit to his authority. When a wife does this and prays for her husband, then God is released to deal powerfully with the husband. I have seen many men dramatically changed by God once the wife began to submit and trust God to change her husband.

Now please don't misunderstand me. I am not saying that a woman should play "Susie Doormat" and passively accept all kinds of nonsense. She has a right to disagree lovingly with her husband and participate with him in the decision-making process. She also should express her needs and desires. But in her heart she should be in submission to him. If she does this, then God's power can enter the relationship and make dramatic changes. This may not happen overnight. It will take time, but God is faithful and He will move.

*28*

## Responsibilities
## of the Wife

U NFORTUNATELY, LIKE MANY modern women, I did not have God-given priorities when we were first married. In the early years of our marriage, my responsibility as a wife was to become a famous actress. In other words, my career was first, and everything else took second place. I had no understanding of, nor did I want to know, what the biblical priorities were.

Just as the man has unique responsibilities, so the wife has been given an entire set of duties that she should perform in order to build a successful marriage. To understand the wife's role, it is important to understand why God created her as well as the unique needs of the male that only she can meet.

The Book of Genesis teaches us that the male feels incomplete without the woman. "And the LORD God said, "It is not good that man should be alone; I will make a helper comparable to him" (Gen. 2:18). God created the woman to a be a helpmate for the man. Recent psychological statistics reveal that men who are divorced or single experience more depression, sickness, heart attacks, alcoholism and early deaths than men who are married. There is something within the male that needs to be in an intimate married relationship with the female.

First, all men since the Fall are insecure in the depths of their being. They spend a great deal of time and energy attempting to prove themselves through sports, business accomplishments, career goals, projects and other things. Men have an innate need to feel that they have conquered something or done something to prove their manhood.

In addition, men have deep ego-centered needs that need to be reinforced regularly. As such, men are attracted to women who make them feel important, significant and powerful. Men like to feel like real men, and the woman who knows how to release that in a man is a wise woman.

God understood the unique psychology of men when He created them. This is why Ephesians 5:33 says to "let the wife see that she respects her husband." A man needs to feel important and worthy of respect, and it is the wife's duty to give her husband this respect.

Let's take a look at the responsibilities of the wife.

### Responsibility 1: The wife is to be submissive to her husband.

In many places the Bible clearly outlines the need for wives to be submissive to their husbands (1 Pet. 3:1; Eph. 5:22; Col. 3:18). God created the marriage relationship to be a rich and wonderful blessing. However, in order for that to happen, both the man and the woman must be in divine order. For the wife, submission is the foundation for a good marriage.

### Responsibility 2: The wife must respect her husband.

There is an expression that people will rise to the level of your expectations, either positive or negative. God calls the wife to respect her husband (Eph. 5:33). This respect is not to be given out only when the husband deserves it. The wife is to respect her husband even if he makes mistakes, fails and stumbles in growth. There is a powerful spiritual principle at work here: If the wife respects her husband even if he does not deserve it at times, she will release him to be everything God created him to be. However, if the wife violates this principle, she can actually hinder the husband's growth and block his growth spiritually.

Proverbs 14:1 says, "The wise woman builds her house, but the foolish pulls it down with her hands." When a woman disrespects her husband through her words or attitude, she is pulling her own house down. There may be cases where the husband is way out of line and may not actually deserve respect. This does not mean that the wife cannot disagree, counsel and correct her husband. But as a general rule, the wife is to respect her husband even if he doesn't always deserve it. In the same way, the husband is to love his wife even when she is unlovely.

### Responsibility 3: The wife is to praise her husband.

The wife is to actively build up her husband and encourage him. She is to seek ways to strengthen, uplift, edify and empower him with her words. These are not to be phony and meaningless words. Proverbs 25:11 says, "A word fitly spoken is like apples of gold in settings of silver." The wife is to use her tongue wisely. There is something about the male psyche that needs consistent, regular and repeated praise.

Women need to understand that their words can set a man free or devastate him. Men are primarily ego-driven, and they need to feel that their efforts, hard work, sacrifice and toil are for a reason. Businesses and corporations that have a real handle on people skills know the importance of rewards and recognition as a means of stimulating better performance. In the same way, the wife must regularly build up and praise her husband.

Careless words spoken by the wife in times of anger and frustration can create strongholds in a man's life that can take many years to undo. Both the man and the woman must remember that God is going to hold all of us accountable for every word that we speak down here on earth.

In Matthew 12:36 Jesus Christ said, "But I say to you that for every idle word men may speak, they will give account of it in the day of judgment."

### Responsibility 4: The wife is to be the lover of her husband.

The wife is to be readily available to her husband sexually. First Corinthians 7:2–9 gives instructions to the husband and wife never to deny themselves sexually to one another unless it is mutually agreed upon. For many men the wife's sexual availability is a sign of love to them. Women must never use sex as a punishment or reward. Many men need regular sexual release as a means of dealing with business pressures, stress or anxiety. Women must understand that often in times of difficulty and stress men need to have sex more—not less—often. The woman must be sensitive to her husband's sexual needs. In the sexual area she must make herself attractive and treat her husband with respect.

This does not mean that the husband is free to take advantage of his wife or use her as some kind of sexual object with no regard for her feelings, emotions or energy level. But it does mean that the husband and wife must prioritize and make time for loving sexual expression. (I'll give more teaching on this topic in the following chapter in this book.)

### Responsibility 5: The wife is to be an intercessor for her husband and family.

The wife has responsibilities spiritually, also. She is to take an active role in praying for her husband and household. Perhaps nothing is as important as a wife who regularly prays for her husband and children. The success, prosperity, favor and release that is brought about by a praying wife is absolutely amazing. Shirley Dobson, the wife of James Dobson of Focus on the Family, found that taking on her role as the intercessor for her husband and family produced amazing results.

A great role model for prayer is Edith Schaeffer, wife of Dr. Francis Schaeffer, the founder of L'Abri and a world renowned philosopher-theologian. She writes in her book *A Celebration of Marriage* that she learned early in her marriage to pray for her the ministry of her husband.

> For me, I felt my very big responsibility (along with caring for Priscilla) was to never stop praying for Fran as he preached. I felt keenly that it was up to me to pray for the power of the Holy Spirit, for the message to really touch not only others but the speaker himself. "Speak to him, and through him" was not just a formula of prayer; it became the cry of my heart. This was to continue through the years, and it was very, very possible and practical for me to continue no matter what, even if we had just had a "fight" of some sort before he spoke.[1]

# 29

# Meeting Your
# Husband's
# Sexual Needs

W<small>E HAVE ALL</small> heard about a man leaving his wife for another woman. In fact, today it is not uncommon for a woman to leave her husband for another man. Sometimes men and women leave their marriage partners because of pure selfishness or lust. But many times men and women become unfaithful to their marriage partners because their needs are not getting met. Instead of working through the marriage problems and believing God for healing and restoration, they listen to the counsel of our society or the lies of a very real devil and choose a sinful affair or divorce.

It is not God's will for men and women to leave their marriage partners in order to seek fulfillment elsewhere.

God wants men and women to work through their problems and build better marriages. Statistics tell us that people who leave their present marriage partners for another simply bring their existing problems into the new relationship. In other words, they don't solve their problems. They just bring the same old problems into the new relationship.

In any marriage, both the man and woman need to accept their responsibility to do things that can strengthen the relationship. In this book, we have already shown men what they can do to be better husbands. But there are many things a wife can do to be a better wife. Just as a man is responsible to do things in order to meet his wife's needs, so a woman is responsible to do things that will meet her husband's needs. When a woman fails to do these things, she is weakening the marriage relationship and letting a guard down around her marriage. The enemy then can come in and tempt her husband. Both husbands and wives must diligently guard against passivity in their marriage and fight for their relationship! Marriages that are neglected eventually die, and this is never God's will for a relationship.

One key area in a marriage relationship is the area of sexual needs. As I pointed out in the previous chapter, the vast majority of men need regular sexual release and sexual attention from their wives. When a wife fails to meet her husband's sexual needs, she negatively affects his psychological and emotional state. The rest of this chapter is devoted to the practical ways a wife can meet her husband's needs in this area.

## What Men Want From Women Sexually

Every married man wants his wife to be his lover. He wants to be admired by his wife, and he wants his wife to be sexually turned on by him. A man wants his wife to dress attractively, to keep herself looking good and to enjoy being with him. Let's face it—women instinctively know how to make their man feel special. When you were courting you knew just how to act in order to make him feel special and keep him interested in you. The problem is that after a period of time many wives neglect their men and take them for granted.

In short, a man needs his wife to be a lover and friend as well as a helpmate and a mother to his children. Please don't misunderstand me. I am not saying that a wife should become a sex object or pretend to be some kind of "hooker." There is a vast difference. God did not create women to be sexually used by men in a lustful and insensitive manner. But God did create a wife to be a man's lover. A healthy sexual relationship between a man and a woman should be fun and mutually pleasurable.

A wife must make herself physically and sexually attractive to her husband and devote time to exciting lovemaking. In the real world of raising children, two-income homes and the energy-draining activities of daily living, finding the time for romance, sex and love can often be a real challenge. However, the challenge is not insurmountable. The husband and wife must make time for love, intimacy and romance.

## THE FRUMPY WIFE SYNDROME

I have just given birth to three children in a year and a half. I am exhausted, and overweight. I have three children in diapers, a house to clean, and meals to fix. I look in the mirror and say, "Oh, no, the frump is here."

—KRISTINA

That is exactly how my wife felt for quite a while after the birth of our three children. As I talk about the "Frumpy Wife Syndrome," I think it is important to say that a lot of what we call the "Frumpy Wife Syndrome" is due to the fact that women are just plain burned out from carrying a load that God never designed for them to carry in the first place. Our entire society is built around both men and women working. But add to that the pressures of women trying to be mothers and wives, and you have created an unbearable burden for women. Many women are on the verge of total collapse from exhaustion—and their husbands and society expect them to be a fashion plate.

Somewhere in this mess there has to be a balance. Men have a strong need for their wives to be as attractive as possible. During the courtship period, women prioritize looking good, having their hair just right and being as attractive as possible. Men feel that women begin to take them for granted after they get married and develop the Frumpy Wife syndrome.

In all honesty, some women have a tendency to let

themselves go after they are married. I think subconsciously they feel that they have bought and own the man; therefore, they can afford to let themselves go a bit. If we are honest, all of us in our sinful human nature have a tendency to take our mates for granted once we are married. It is important that both men and women fight against this tendency. There are a lot of guys sitting around in their underwear and some old T-shirt.

Women need to understand that it is very important to their husband that they make a reasonable effort at making themselves look attractive as a way of blessing their mate. At the same time, men need to understand that modern women have incredible pressures on them and are often exhausted and at the end of their rope. It is insensitive to have unrealistic expectations about our wives. Both men and women need to find a middle ground in this area.

## WHAT ABOUT 1 PETER?

As you read this chapter you may have thought, *What about that passage in 1 Peter about fixing your hair and putting on jewelry? How does that fit with being attractive for my husband?* To answer those questions, let's review the passage in question:

> Do not let your adornment be merely outward—arranging the hair, wearing gold, or putting on fine apparel—rather let it be the hidden person of the heart, with the incorruptible beauty of a gentle and

quiet spirit, which is very precious in the sight of God. For in this manner, in former times, the holy women who trusted in God also adorned themselves, being submissive to their own husbands, as Sarah obeyed Abraham, calling him lord, whose daughters you are if do good and are not afraid with any terror.

—1 Peter 3:3–6

Now it's easy to read that passage and completely misunderstand what it is saying, as many people have done in religious circles throughout the years. This passage of Scripture is not calling for women to become weird "Plain Janes" who bow their heads all the time and never wear any makeup. Sad to say, many religious groups have gotten the false idea that women should walk around looking ugly and never saying a word.

The Bible is really saying that Christian women are not to place their emphasis on the outer appearance only, as the women of the world do. Women who do not know God are often consumed with concern about their appearance, makeup, clothing and status symbols, like designer fashions and jewelry, while they completely ignore their spiritual development. Women of faith are first concerned with being women who are in a right relationship with Jesus Christ and submissive to their husbands. When these things are in order, then a Christian woman can make herself look attractive in a way with dignity that befits a woman of God.

201

## Avoiding the Superwoman Syndrome

Now that we have listed some of the wives' responsibilities, it is important to clarify what has been said so that we do not put any woman in bondage or place unnecessary burdens on them. God is not calling the wife to be a superwoman, which is what society seems to be telling women these days. A lot of the female role models presented by our society are totally unrealistic and end up stressing out the average woman.

Women are confronted with the exercise video where an attractive twenty-year-old who has never had children teaches how to keep in shape, with the movie star who had extensive cosmetic surgery and her own personal trainer who shares her secrets of beauty, and with the female network newscaster who spends her off hours at an exotic spa getting deep tissue massages and facials while having her nails done. These lifestyles of the rich and famous only place unrealistic demands on ordinary women.

God is not expecting women to live up to some impossible standard of perfection. But God does expect the woman who has kids or maybe works to spend some time making herself attractive to her husband. This is part of her ministry to her husband and family.

## A Word of Caution

There are some men who because of their own self-centeredness and carnality place impossible demands upon their wives. These men are not thankful for the wives that

God has given them and falsely expect their wives to be perfect in every way. Men like this tend to put tremendous emotional pressure on their wives to live up to their unrealistic demands for physical perfection and sexual gratification. This puts wives on a "treadmill experience" that only leads to deep frustration and resentment.

A wife is responsible to do her best in making herself attractive for her husband. But in the real world, some men (and even some Christian men) are unthankful and are perfectionists. A wife needs discernment here.

Nowhere does the Bible call for a women to kill herself trying to please her husband's unrealistic demands. As such, a word of caution is necessary here.

# Section VII
# Romantic Reality Checks

*30*

# Men's and Women's Fantasies About Marriage

Before the wedding, both men and women have fantasies about what the marriage relationship will be like. Since men and women are different, the nature of their fantasies is also different. This chapter will look at those fantasies and help you to keep them from undermining your marriage.

### THE PLAYMATE FANTASY

Basically, a lot of men think that when they get married, they will share life together with a woman who will be someone who will laugh at their jokes and with whom they can have a good time. This woman will also bear their children—and take care of them—and be available for sex any time they want it. I will label this male fantasy and the many variations that stem from it the *Playmate Fantasy.*

The Playmate Fantasy stems from things like Hugh Hefner's *Playboy Magazine.* The *Playboy* philosophy promotes the idea that women are the sexual playthings of men. It is a very destructive idea that is responsible for rape, sexual molestation and abuse of women in our culture.

Although a man may have been a virgin until he was married and never read a pornographic magazine like *Playboy* or *Penthouse* in his life, the ideas promoted by these magazines have permeated our popular culture. The idea of the woman as a sex object or "playmate" is deeply ingrained in the consciousness of men around the world. Even though many men would reject that philosophy consciously, some of its effects have managed to become a part of the way we think as a culture.

Everything from football cheerleaders and the *Sports Illustrated* swimsuit issue to the way cars and beer are sold on television suggests that women are to be the playthings of men. Even the Christian man often has the idea embedded in his subconscious that his wife is to be not only a mother to his children and a companion to him but also a kind of sexual playmate. This message is communicated subliminally in magazines, television shows, movies and commercials. This idea, which is very much from the "world spirit," has set up strongholds in the minds of many men, and it needs to be dismantled by the Word of God.

Please do not misunderstand me. I am not arguing for some kind of nonbiblical prudery. God created sexuality for men and women to enjoy thoroughly. In fact, it was God who created the orgasm—not *Playboy* or *Penthouse*. God has blessed us with the joy, wonder and excitement of sexual expression. Genesis 2:18 says, "And the LORD God said, 'It is not good that man should be alone; I will make a helper comparable to him.'" Notice that God did not say, "I will make a playmate for him." Although God intended married men and women to enjoy a sexual relationship, as seen in Genesis 2:24 where He states, "...and they shall become one flesh" (which refers to them becoming one through sexual intercourse), He created the woman to be a full and complete person in her own right as well as a spiritual, emotional and sexual companion.

Jesus Christ calls men to love their wives as Christ loved the church. This cannot happen if a man perceives his wife to be some kind of object for his own gratification. Men are to lay down their lives for their wives and serve them. In the proper context they are free to enjoy a rich sexual life with their wives. But they are never to hold the idea—even subtly—that a woman can be used as an object of sexual or emotional gratification.

## THE KNIGHT IN SHINING ARMOR FANTASY

Women also have a fantasy of what the ideal marriage relationship should be based on a popular cultural fantasy that I have labeled the *Knight in Shining Armor Philosophy*. Although women usually don't read magazines like *Playboy* and *Penthouse*, soap operas, romantic novels and women's magazines promote their own fantasy in which a rich, handsome, powerful man becomes the perfect, sensitive, romantic lover who meets all their needs in life.

A casual glance at a soap opera will show a parade of dashing doctors, lawyers, architects and professionals along with an occasional rebel such as a rock 'n' roll star who sweeps a woman off her feet and showers her with flowers, love notes, romantic trips, bubble baths, champagne wishes and caviar dreams. In this Knight in Shining Armor Fantasy, the woman gets all her emotional needs met by this "perfect lover" until some conflict comes along. Often seen on the cover of romantic novels is a strong male figure, such as a military leader, who amorously embraces a woman and kisses her passionately. The idea is that this "perfect male" will come along, sweep her off her feet and provide the leadership, protection and emotional satisfaction that she desires.

This Knight in Shining Armor Fantasy is equally as dangerous as the Playmate Fantasy because it upholds an unrealistic view of a "perfect man" and selfishly demands that a husband be a knight in shining armor who is always sensitive, forever strong and always protecting her perfectly.

In both the man's and woman's fantasy, conflicts inevitably arise as both partners do not meet their mate's idealized expectations. The Christian woman may attempt to Christianize this subconscious fantasy and make her husband a combination of Billy Graham and Michael Douglas. In this fantasy, the husband is both the spiritual giant and the romantic movie star.

But the point is, these are idealized images. Ultimately each spouse needs to let go of the fantasies and enjoy his or her mate for who that person really is.

# 31

# Love by Faith
# and the Feelings
# Will Follow

T HE MARRIAGE RELATIONSHIP has different phases. In the
early days of what can be called the courtship
phase, there is a powerful release of romantic and sexual
energy. Please don't misunderstand what I am saying. I am
not saying that the courtship should involve sexual relations—because it should not. Sexual expression is to be
reserved until after the two people have become married.
But in the courtship phase, sexuality plays a powerful role
as the two lovers wait expectantly for the consummation
of their relationship.

However, the romantic high will not last forever. While
powerful romantic feelings continue to exist in any
healthy marriage, these feelings also deepen and mature.

Strong sexual urges and romantic feelings will continue to exist if the marriage relationship is properly cultivated. But, there will also be "dry" times where we may actually dislike our mates. It is during those times that we must learn to love our mates by faith and not feelings.

In any marriage there will be times when we simply do not feel like loving our mates. In fact, we may actually feel cold and distant from them. When this happens in the world, people believe that "the thrill is gone," and they begin to look outside of their marriage for romance and excitement.

However, God requires that in these dry times we love our mates by faith—not feelings. In other words, we say kind things and do loving things for our partners even though we may not feel like it.

What happens is that as we love our mates by faith, we discover that the romantic and loving feelings will follow. In a sense, loving our marriage partners even when we don't feel like it primes the romantic pump, and soon the love and intimacy spring up in our relationship. In a very real sense, if we plant seeds of kindness, love, tenderness and romance in the relationship, these seeds will blossom.

We are not to wait for our marriage partners to love us. We are to love them and cultivate them and believe God to produce a harvest of intimacy. Remember, the Christian is not in the marriage relationship alone. He or she has God as a partner, and He is well able to deal with our mate if we are praying for our partner and doing what we are supposed to be doing.

In loving by faith, God has put the ball in the man's court. It is the man who is primarily responsible for creating the romantic climate in the marriage. If men properly love and treat their wives with tenderness, dignity and respect, then the romantic feelings and sparks begin to fly. A man who pays attention to his wife's needs soon discovers that his wife pays attention to his needs. Women are sexually responsive to men who are responsive to their needs. It is up to men to set the romantic tone of the marriage.

## FORGIVENESS

Dry times are likely to come when unforgiveness has entered the relationship. No matter how much in love two people are, they are going to say things that hurt and bruise each other. Ephesians 4:32 says, "And be kind to one another, tenderhearted, forgiving one another, even as God in Christ forgave you." Any couple that has been married a while has been able to do so because they have learned to forgive one another.

When a man and a woman become intimate emotionally, spiritually and sexually, they know each other at the deepest levels of their lives. They know each other's insecurities, fears, apprehensions and "hot buttons."

When an argument occurs, both marriage partners have at their disposal emotional "nuclear weapons." Wives know exactly how to "go in for the kill" if they want to get back at or wound their husbands. Husbands know exactly what to do or say that will really hurt their wives.

Unfortunately, our flesh gets involved when we are upset, hurt and annoyed, and we wound our mates as no stranger can. Of course, this is sin and absolutely wrong, but when tempers flare, unkind words can easily be spoken.

Once those unkind words are spoken, they are impossible to take back again. The cutting remarks and hurtful words can go off in our heads like pinball machines and bounce around in our heart and soul for a long, long time. The only way we can be healed of the pain and bondage those words can bring is to truly forgive the person who offended us. We need to forgive them even if they offend us over and over again.

In and of ourselves we do not have the capacity for this kind of forgiveness. But if we go to God in prayer and ask Him to give us His supernatural power to forgive someone, He will. If we rely on His Spirit, then we can really let go of those hurts and forgive others, no matter how deeply they have hurt us.

# 32

# Romantic
# Reality Checks

M ANY COUPLES ACT like Ken and Barbie when they are first married—at least before they have kids.

### Romantic Reality Check #1
### Kiss Barbie good-bye

Then Barbie gets pregnant and loses her Barbie-doll figure. In addition, now that Barbie has kids to take care of, she can't spend all her time fixing herself up and looking pretty. Many guys (Ken) expect their wives to be Barbie forever. Well, life isn't that way. Both Ken and Barbie get older, gain weight and get gray hair. Part of life is learning how to deal with it!

### *Romantic Reality Check #2*
### *Too pooped for passion*

Our society promotes an unrealistic view of sex and romance through television, film and magazines. In this fantasy world of idealized sex and romance, everybody is young, attractive and rich. The reality is that in the real world it is not always like that.

A lot of people have to work long hours at their jobs. All of us get older, lose our figures and in general just don't measure up to Hollywood's perfect world.

In addition, having children, cleaning house and doing all the other things it takes to stay alive make a lot of us too pooped for passion! Unfortunately, many men pressure their wives to look, act and dress perfectly because they have an unrealistic and emotionally immature view of romance. Sex and romance in the real world involves keeping the passion alive in a marriage despite the kids, jobs, wrinkles, pounds and fatigue.

Both men and women need to cultivate a thankful spirit for their mates and learn how to appreciate them as the years go by. If either the man or the woman has an unrealistic expectation of what the relationship should be either romantically, emotionally or sexually, then they may damage the good but imperfect relationship that is truly possible for them. We need to be careful not to allow the materialistic and idolatrous mind-set of our day to enter our marriage. We need to be truly thankful for the marriage partner God has given us.

217

### Romantic Reality Check #3
### Tough times come

The hard, cold facts about marriage are that there will be times when we will actually be disgusted by and even feel contempt for our mates. Every single one of us has times when we are disgusted by, hate and are angry at ourselves. So why do we think that we can live with someone else for five, ten, fifteen, twenty years or more and not experience those same negative feelings?

Marriage is not just about flowers, passion, holding hands and intimate conversations. Marriage is about walking through some pretty tough times together and dealing with pressures, challenges and problems. I don't want to burst some bubbles, but kids throw up, people have constipation, get sick, have bad breath or at the very least a bad hair day!

If you are expecting that romantic or the *eros* kind of love will get you through these times, you are in for a rude awakening. There is nothing wrong with *eros* in a marriage. But you can't build a lifetime on *eros*. Every married couple needs to learn how to walk in the power of the Holy Spirit and to be filled with the *agape* kind of love. It is only the *agape* kind of love that will make a marriage last, and this love is only produced by being filled regularly with the Holy Spirit.

The reality is that there are going to be times when your mate literally turns your stomach because of the pressures of life, his or her idiosyncrasies, habits or just plain weariness. The only thing that will help you in times like this is coming to Jesus Christ, confessing your negative feelings and asking God to fill you with fresh love for your mate. If you do this, you will find that the *agape* kind of love begins to fill your heart—and don't be surprised if the *eros* comes back, too.

Remember that true love is not based on feelings. Ask God regularly to give you His love for your mate. Cleanse your heart of bitterness and resentment. Love by faith, and the feelings will follow.

......................................................................

# 33

# Keep Talking

T ALKING TOGETHER IS a key feature of a successful marriage, but good communication is often undermined by a lack of understanding. Below are some guidelines to help you communicate successfully, based on the following two key scriptures:

> Let no unwholesome word proceed from your mouth, but only such a word as is good for edification.
>
> —EPHESIANS 4:29, NAS

> For this cause a man shall leave his father and mother, and shall cleave to his wife; and the two shall become one flesh.
>
> —EPHESIANS 5:31, NAS

## EIGHT PRINCIPLES OF COMMUNICATION

### *Communication Principle 1:*
### *Keep the in-laws out of the marriage.*

One of the basic foundations of any good marriage is that a husband and wife do not allow their in-laws to control their marriage. (It's the principle of "leave and cleave.") Parents have a tendency of taking sides.

### *Communication Principle 2:*
### *Maintain a positive outlook.*

In marriage you need always to maintain a positive outlook. "Is the cup half full or half empty?" If you focus on the half-empty part of any situation, you're going to become negative and depressed. Kristina was a school teacher, and she always told her class that they were the smartest class she had ever had. Kristina worked in an inner-city school, and there were some very real problems. However, she helped her students to see themselves as extraordinary because that was how God created them. We also need to help our spouses see themselves as extraordinary, because this will enable them to accomplish extraordinary things. We release or limit God in our lives by our belief system, perception and attitudes. The Bible states that as a man thinks in his heart, so is he. (See Proverbs 23:7.) What we expect from our mates and believe about them often become true. It is important that we see them as God sees them.

### Communication Principle 3:
### Say, "I am sorry."

We should be quick to admit to our mates when we are wrong and never be afraid to say "I am sorry."

### Communication Principle 4:
### Be kind and compassionate.

Colossians 3:12 states, "Put on a heart of compassion, kindness, humility, gentleness and patience" (NAS). Remember, conflict is not one-sided. Try to understand your responsibility in any conflict and how you may have hurt your spouse. Go before the Lord and confess that you participated in weakening the marriage. Also, you may need to go to your spouse and ask for forgiveness. Try to see any conflict through your spouse's eyes—not just your own.

End every day with a clean slate. Don't collect all the offenses throughout the day or week or years. If we're hurt, we are more alert to the flaws of the offender. Emotionally we feel estranged; physically we don't want to be touched by that person; spiritually we close out that person. We need to be on guard against allowing walls to be built between us and our mates because this is how the devil can destroy a marriage.

### Communication Principle 5:
### Protect your marriage's privacy.

Unfortunately, society does not require any education to be a husband or wife. Since we have no training in marriage, we rely solely on the training we observed in the home as a child. We enter marriage knowing about sex from TV, movies and on the street. Our home example may have been insufficient. As such, we may be tempted to talk about our marriage problems publicly. But this undermines our mates and opens us up to all kinds of ungodly counsel.

1. Don't communicate to strangers what you're trying to say to your spouse.
2. Don't bring your problems to the public forum, for example, talking to neighbors, relatives, strangers and so on. This breaks trust and attempts to undermine the spouse. If we do this, our spouse will feel "ganged up on" by family members—his/her family vs. me.
3. There are always two sides to the problem. Although one person appears to be the lamb and the other the lion, take a closer look at the lamb. The lamb may be crushing the lion's toe, which makes him roar loudly. The lion appears to be the problem but he/she is just displaying the pain the lamb is putting on him/her.
4. The person who does nothing in a relationship seems to win. Imagine a scenario where one of the marriage partners is a slob, and the other partner wants his or her mate to clean up or be neat. If the messy partner does nothing except watch TV, the other partner may be doing all the work—emotionally and physically. This can create conflicts. On a superficial level, the neat

and orderly spouse looks like the "bad guy," but in reality the fact that the messy partner doesn't seem to care about neatness is creating the problems.

### *Communication Principle 6:*
### *Communicate gently with backslidden or unsaved mates.*

Perhaps your spouse is always attacking you for your Christianity, saying he or she worships God his or her own way and has his or her own Jesus, yet he or she never reads the Word or goes to church. This spouse seeks out friends who have been burned out by Christianity or who have rejected Jesus Christ in their lives and gathers emotional support for his or her "backslidden state" or hardness of heart toward God.

In these situations and others, the "on-fire" Christian has been put on stage. Your mate, friends, family, coworkers and neighbors will often put your life under a microscope, looking for any fault or inconsistency in your Christian walk. Everything you do publicly will be looked at through critical, pharisaical eyes.

The key here is not to try to be perfect. You will only have a nervous breakdown if you do. Call upon God's grace and mercy in these situations. Remember that it is in the nitty-gritty circumstances of life that you will have an opportunity to be a witness for Jesus Christ to your mate and others. Pray and fast for strongholds to be broken down. In these situations learn to communicate gently with your voice. The tone of voice is crucial. With close relatives the slightest wrong tone with the voice will give them ammunition with which to crucify you for years. It's not what you say—it's how you say it. When trying to communicate to people who have hardened their hearts toward Jesus Christ, remember to act wisely in all things. Your speech, conduct, dress and appearance are all important.

### Communication Principle 7:
### Don't accumulate offenses.

In the course of any marriage relationship, our spouses will do and say things that "tick us off" and make us angry. We need to be careful that we do not store up these offenses in our spirit and then explode against our mates at some later time. It is especially important that we resolve these issues before we go to sleep each night. This is why the apostle Paul said, "Be angry, and do not sin: do not let the sun go down on your wrath" (Eph. 4:26).

### Communication Principle 8:
### Learn to be a good listener.

I have had the privilege of teaching about marriage through many platforms—books, magazine articles, radio and television seminars across the nation. In addition, I host a live daily radio talk show when I regularly counsel people about their lives and marriages. However, in all honesty, I have discovered it is quite easy to be "on" when the spotlight is on you. It is quite another thing to "walk your talk" when no one is looking. With this in my mind, let me relate the words my wife said to me one evening when we were driving to church.

Kristina was going through some intense difficulties at work, and she was attempting to talk to me about them. I had the annoying habit of saying to her "Right, right" every few moments in order to let her know that I was really listening to her. Now in reality, I was more interested in what I had to say rather than really listening. Finally, in exasperation she exclaimed, "You know, you would make a lousy psychologist!"

I answered back, "What do you mean by that?"

She said, "You don't know how to listen!"

*Great,* I thought to myself. *Here I am giving her my time and really trying to help by listening, and she calls me a poor listener and a lousy psychologist.* But after I had reflected on her remarks for a while, I realized that I was not being the attentive listener she needed me to be. I needed to get my own ego out of the way and really tune in to her needs.

Men often make the mistake of taking things at face value when listening to what their wives say. A wife may say one thing, but often she has a deeper meaning and is trying to communicate something else. In good communication, men need to know how to develop a "third ear" and listen to their inner voice. In other words, behind my wife's words, I need to listen for what she is really trying to communicate to me.

Here are a few principles men can use to be effective listeners to their wives:

1.  Really focus on what she has to say rather than just waiting for an opportunity to interrupt her and give her a lecture.
2.  Listen with a "third ear" and inner voice to hear what she is really saying behind the words.
3.  When it is appropriate, rephrase what she is saying back to her and ask her if that is what she meant.
4.  Do not attempt to edit, censor or change what she has said. Give her the freedom to completely express herself without fearing your judgment or opinions.

# 34

# How to Fall in
# Love All Over Again

KRISTINA AND I were vacationing on the island of
Maui a number of years ago. You could take a
sunset cruise on a small yacht called the *Genesis* where
you were served steak or fish while a guitarist played
romantic music as you sailed off into the tropical sunset.
After eating the delicious dinner, Kris and I looked up
from the deck to watch the endless stars in the sky as we
sailed effortlessly around this island paradise. We called
this experience "The Maui Light Show" because the sky is
so clear that it seems as if you can see forever.

In an environment like this, it doesn't take long to jump-
start any marriage. You very quickly remember the reasons
why you fell in love in the first place. The powerful

chemistry that brought you together in the first place starts to go into high gear. Every man and woman who fall in love and get married start from a place of genuine romance. One of the reasons that marriages go sour is that the grind of the daily routine, conflicts, arguments, stress, money, jobs, children and life in general squelches those romantic feelings. They can get so deeply buried that you seem to forget why you married the other person in the first place.

In any marriage it's important to remember the attributes of the other person who brought you together in the first place.

- What exactly were the reasons that you fell in love with your husband or wife in the first place?

- What exactly was it that attracted you to that person?

- What made you want to marry and spend the rest of your life together? Try the following exercise.

List the ten most important things that attracted you to your husband.

1. _____
2. _____
3. _____
4. _____
5. _____
6. _____
7. _____
8. _____
9. _____
10. _____

List the ten most important things that attracted you to your wife.

1. _____
2. _____
3. _____
4. _____
5. _____
6. _____
7. _____
8. _____
9. _____
10. _____

## YOU CAN HAVE A WONDERFUL MARRIAGE

You can have a wonderful marriage—not a perfect marriage, but a blessed marriage. The key to a successful marriage is inviting God into it. Many Christians want God to bless their marriages, but they are not willing to obey Him. A wonderful marriage is not built on sex, love and romance. A successful marriage is built on Jesus Christ.

We have shared our own personal testimony and many biblical principles regarding marriage. The rest is up to you. There is no magic formula for a successful marriage. But we have found one principle that works: Cry out to God! No matter where you are in your life or marriage, cry out to God! He will hear you, and He will answer you. Cast aside your doubts, unbelief and smallness of heart and mind. God is the Creator and Master of the Universe. He has the power to make your marriage work. Cry out to Him!

> Call to Me, and I will answer you, and show you great and mighty things, which you do not know.
>
> —JEREMIAH 33:3

YOUR FRIENDS IN CHRIST,
PAUL AND KRISTINA MCGUIRE

# Notes

## Chapter 2
### Imperfect People Who Love Each Other

1. Barbara Dafoe Whitehead, "Dan Quayle Was Right," *Atlantic Monthly,* and Jerry Adler, "Growing Up Scared," *Newsweek,* January 1994.

## Chapter 3
### A Romance at the Beginning of Time

1. *The Spirit-Filled Life Bible,* gen. ed. Jack W. Hayford, Litt.D. (Nashville,: Thomas Nelson Publishers, 1991), 5.

## Chapter 4
### The Marriage Covenant

1. *The Spirit-Filled Life Bible,* 29.

## Chapter 6
### The Myth of the Perfect Marriage

1. *The Spirit-Filled Life Bible,* 1260.
2. Francis Schaeffer, *Complete Works of Francis A. Schaeffer, vol. 3, True Spirituality,* (Westchester, IL: Crossway Books, 1982), 328.

## Chapter 18
### Sex, Society and Statistics

1. Ann Landers, *Los Angeles Daily News,* September 25, 1994.

## Chapter 23
### Responsibilities of the Husband

1. John Whitehead, *Religious Apartheid* (Chicago: Moody Press, 1994), 235.

## Chapter 26
### The Role of the Woman

1. Whitehead, *Religious Apartheid,* 235.
2. *The Spirit-Filled Life Bible,* note on Ephesians 5:21–22, 1795.
3. *The Spirit-Filled Life Bible,* 1911.
4. Edith Schaeffer, *A Celebration of Marriage* (Grand Rapids, MI: Baker Books, 1994) 32–33.

## Chapter 28
### Responsibilities of the Wife

1. Schaeffer, Edith, *A Celebration of Marriage,* 57.

# About the Authors

Paul McGuire is the host of the live radio talk show Home Builders, whose goal is to strengthen marriage and families. He is a member of the faculty of the Kings College and Seminary of which Dr. Jack Hayford is the chancellor. Paul is an internationally known conference speaker and the author of ten books, which include *Countdown to Armageddon* from Creation House. He hosted the End of the Age Conference with Dr. Pat Robertson at the Christian Broadcasting Network. Paul is a widely known expert on marriages and families who has been interviewed by many national magazines, radio and television shows. Prior to writing books, Paul produced feature films in Hollywood. He has been married to his wife, Kristina, for over twenty-three years. They live in Southern California with their three children.

Kristina McGuire is an author, conference speaker and artist. Kristina starred in several feature films and co-starred with Tom Selleck in *The Shadow Riders*. Kristina attended the Juilliard School of Drama in New York City and starred in several off-Broadway plays in New York City and Los Angeles, including *Bleacher Bums*. She has studied with Milton Katselas and is an author and illustrator of children's books. Kristina is a *magna cum laude* graduate of the University of Utah.

*To receive a free newsletter and to find out more about the McGuire's ministry, visit their Web site at:*
*www.paulmcguire.com*

*Or write:*

PAUL MCGUIRE
P.O. Box 803001
Santa Clarita, CA 91380-3001

## ATTENTION CALIFORNIA RESIDENTS!

Paul McGuire can be heard every weekday from
2–3:30 p.m. as the host of Home Builders.
Tune in to KBRT AM 740 broadcasting from Costa
Mesa, California.

# *You* can experience more of *God's grace & love!*

*I*f you would like free information on how you can know God more deeply and experience His grace, love and power more fully in your life, simply write or e-mail us. We'll be delighted to send you information that will be a blessing to you.

To check out other titles from **Creation House** that will impact your life, be sure to visit your local Christian bookstore, or call this toll-free number:

## 1-800-599-5750

*For free information from Creation House:*

**CREATION HOUSE**
600 Rinehart Rd.
Lake Mary, FL 32746
www.creationhouse.com

# Your Walk With God Can Be Even Deeper...

**W**ith *Charisma* magazine, you'll be informed and inspired by the features and stories about what the Holy Spirit is doing in the lives of believers today.

### Each issue:
- Brings you exclusive world-wide reports to rejoice over.
- Keeps you informed on the latest news from a Christian perspective.
- Includes miracle-filled testimonies to build your faith.
- Gives you access to relevant teaching and exhortation from the most respected Christian leaders of our day.

## Call 1-800-829-3346 for 3 FREE trial issues
Offer #AOACHB

If you like what you see, then pay the invoice of $22.97 (**saving over 51% off the cover price**) and receive 9 more issues (12 in all). Otherwise, write "cancel" on the invoice, return it, and owe nothing.

## Experience the Power of Spirit-Led Living